PASSAGES
An Intermediate/Advanced Writing Book

PASSAGES

An Intermediate/Advanced Writing Book

Len Fox

Brooklyn College of the City University of New York

HBJ

HARCOURT BRACE JOVANOVICH, INC.

New York • San Diego • Chicago • San Francisco • Atlanta
London • Sydney • Toronto

To those who have taught me,
more than anyone else,
about living and loving life:
Ginny, Amy, Lucy

TO THE TEACHER

This book is concerned with "passages" of different sorts. For one thing, there are reading passages at the beginning of each chapter, which I hope you and your students will find worth discussing and writing about. Secondly, the reading passages and writing assignments in the book are concerned with the "passages" that we make throughout our lifetimes: childhood, going to school, getting a job, joining adult society, forming adult relationships, facing old age, and death. These are stages that we all must pass through. Hence, we should be glad for the chance to read about these stages, to talk about them, to think about them, and to write about them. Finally, we as teachers are concerned that our students make the "passage" from being inexperienced, unskilled writers to being more proficient ones. I hope this book will help.

Model Passages and Writing Assignments

Each chapter begins with a passage that is meant to stimulate thinking and discussion on the "theme" of the chapter (which is related to the larger theme of each section of the book: growing up, education, and so on). The first five chapters have paragraphs as models (two descriptive, one narrative, two opinion and support), and the students are asked to write their own paragraphs at the end of the chapter. In chapter six, the essay is introduced (thesis sentence, introduction, body, conclusion), and the model passages from this point on are essays (two opinion and support, one descriptive, one narrative, one definition, two classification, one comparison). In some chapters, the student is told what type of essay to write (chapter six, opinion and support; chapter eight, problem solution; chapter nine, comparison), but in most chapters, the student is given a choice of different questions which call for different essay types. I have provided sample outlines of the model passages at the beginning of the chapters, outlines in the writing sections of a type of paragraph or essay that students could write, and, in an appendix, additional models (which I wrote myself) based on the sample outlines given at the end of each chapter.

Students should be given ample time to think and to discuss (the crucial "brainstorming" phase) before writing. I strongly encourage students to do an outline before writing, although they don't necessarily have to stick to it exactly in their writing. I feel that a certain amount of invention occurs during the writing process, so we can't necessarily hold ourselves or our students strictly to an outline. The outline is particularly important for students who have difficulty in presenting their ideas in a logical, organized way.

Exercises

I have written this book for English as a second language and basic writing students. Some of the exercises and grammar sections (prepositions, articles, present perfect tense) are specifically intended only for ESL students. These are indicated by an asterisk next to the exercises. But most of the exercises and grammar sections (comprehension questions, sentence ordering, punctuation, proofreading, writing correct sentences, coordination, subordination, subject-verb agreement, use of pronouns, passive verb forms) will be useful for *both* ESL and basic writing students. The sentence ordering exercises and the rhetorical devices sections deal with the recently much discussed topics of cohesion and functional devices. The proofreading exercises (a crucial and much neglected phase of writing) take the students through three steps: errors underlined and indicated in the margin (in chapters 1-3); errors indicated only in the margin (in chapters 4-7); errors indicated only at the top of the passage (in chapters 8-13). Many of the exercises involve students working in pairs or small groups and writing paragraphs with a grammatical focus. This serves the threefold purpose of teaching grammar, teaching writing, and teaching students to communicate and interact with each other (an important aspect, I believe, of what should go on in any classroom).

Evaluation

What happens after the writing assignment is done? Well, there are three things that I consider important. First, students must get the feeling that the teacher has taken their writing and ideas seriously. The teacher can make comments (either in the margin, at the beginning, or at the end of a paper) not only on what is *not* good ("You need an example," "Not true," "Unclear,"), but also on what *is* good ("Good point," "Nice story," "I agree"). Students should feel that the teacher is a sympathetic "listener" and should be encouraged to feel good about their writing and about themselves (at least encouraged enough to feel like going on and doing another writing assignment). In addition, I strongly recommend having students read their papers to each other in small groups, thus giving them an "audience." (During group reading, the teacher can move from group to group, making sure the students' comments are valid and helpful.)

Second, the teacher should first indicate the *major* grammatical errors, allowing the student to see *patterns* of errors (two or three specific types of errors that he or she especially tends to make). This "focused correcting" (not correcting everything) tells students that they must learn the rules governing a particular grammatical area, learn to proofread for this particular type of error, and learn to eliminate it from their writing. The teacher should not overcorrect; overcorrecting simply discourages students, suggesting to them that there is no way they will ever become competent writers.

Third, after content and major grammatical errors have been corrected, I would suggest correcting other, less important errors. We are thus talking about *three* drafts of a paper: a first rough draft, a second draft with content and major grammatical errors corrected, and a third draft with other errors corrected. At Brooklyn College, my colleagues and I are coming to feel that it is better to write fewer essays (maybe eight rather than twelve over a semester), and to do a more thorough job of preparing for and revising/correcting each assignment. In this way, the student is more likely to learn from the preceding assignment how to make the next one better.

Thanks

I wish to express special thanks to the late William A. Pullin, a warm, charming, delightful man whom I had the great pleasure of working with at Harcourt Brace Jovanovich. Thanks also to Al Richards, Andrea Haight, Nancy Shehorn, Lynn Edwards, Tricia Griffith, and Amanda Walker at Harcourt Brace Jovanovich, and especially to Shirley Braun, whose excellent advice played a large role in bringing this book to its final shape. Finally, thanks to Lily Kapili and to my fine colleagues and students at Brooklyn College, who have provided fertile ground for my ideas to grow.

LEN FOX

CONTENTS

To the Teacher   vii

To the Student   xv

Part One: Paragraphs
GROWING UP

1 **A Special Place**   3
   Model: from "Italians in Hell's Kitchen" Mario Puzo   3

   Comprehension Questions   4
   Form   4
   Rhetorical Devices   4
   Grammar and Sentence Structure   5
   Complete Sentences   5
   Sentence Fragments   6
   Run-on Sentences   7
   Punctuation   8
   Writing   10

2 **A Special Person**   13
   Model: from *Blackberry Winter* Margaret Mead   13

   Comprehension Questions   14
   Form   14
   Rhetorical Devices   14
   Grammar and Sentence Structure   15
   Coordination   15
   Sentence Connectors   16

Subordination   18
Writing   20

3 **A Memorable Experience**   **23**
Model: from "Out in Right Field" Peter Candell   **23**

Comprehension Questions   23
Form   24
Rhetorical Devices   24
Grammar and Sentence Structure   24
Adjective Clauses   25
Restrictive and Nonrestrictive Clauses   26
Omitting the Connecting Word   26
Appositives   27
Writing   28

EDUCATION

4 **Memorable Teachers**   **33**
Models: from "Time and Tide" John A. Williams   **33**
from "Education" E. B. White   **33**

Comprehension Questions   34
Form: Topic Sentence and Support   34
Rhetorical Devices   34
Grammar and Sentence Structure   35
Subject-Verb Agreement Review   36
Subject-Verb Agreement: Special Problems   37
Pronoun Agreement   38
Pronoun Reference   39
Writing   41

5 **The Purpose of Education**   **43**
Model: From *On Becoming a Person* Carl R. Rogers   **43**

Comprehension Questions   44
Form   44
Rhetorical Devices   44
Grammar and Sentence Structure   44
Verb Tenses   45
The Present Perfect Tense   47
Other Perfect Tenses   48
Writing   49

Part Two: Essays
JOBS

6 **Getting A Job**   **53**
Model: from *Growing Up Absurd* Paul Goodman   **53**

Comprehension Questions   54
Form: Thesis Sentence and The Essay   54
Rhetorical Devices   56
Grammar and Sentence Structure   56
Articles: The Indefinite Article   57
The Definite Article   58
Writing   60

7 **Money**   **63**
Model: from "Measuring Maculinity by the Size of a Paycheck"
Robert E. Gould   **63**

Comprehension Questions   64
Form   64
Rhetorical Devices   64
Grammar and Sentence Structure   65
Word Forms   66
Sentence Variety   68
Writing   69

PROBLEMS IN SOCIETY

8 **World Problems**   **73**
Model: from "Developing Global Units for Elementary Schools"
Donald Morris   **73**

Comprehension Questions   74
Form   74
Rhetorical Devices   74
Grammar and Sentence Structure   75
Passive Verb Forms   76
Writing   78

9 **Cities**   **81**
Model: from "Dirt, Grime, and Cruel Crowding" Eric Sevareid   **81**

Comprehension Questions   82
Form   82
Rhetorical Devices   83
Grammar and Sentence Structure   84
Comparing with Adjectives and Adverbs   85
Direct Speech and Reported Speech   86
Writing   88

RELATIONSHIPS

10 **The Family**   **91**
Model: from *Future Shock* Alvin Toffler   **91**

Comprehension Questions   92

Form   92
Rhetorical Devices   93
Grammar and Sentence Structure   93
Modal Verbs   94
Writing   96
Introductions and Conclusions   96
An Essay on the Family   98

11 Brotherly Love   101
Model: from *The Art of Loving* Erich Fromm   101

Comprehension Questions   102
Form   102
Rhetorical Devices   103
Grammar and Sentence Structure   103
Conditional Sentences   104
Writing   106

GROWING OLD

12 Facing Death   111
Model: from "Facing Up to Death" Elisabeth Kübler-Ross   111

Comprehension Questions   112
Form   113
Rhetorical Devices   113
Grammar and Sentence Structure   113
Verbals: Infinitives   115
Verbals: Gerunds   115
Conventional Uses of Infinitives and Gerunds   115
Noun Phrases   116
Writing   118

13 Memories Live On   121
Model: from *Blackberry Winter* Margaret Mead   121

Comprehension Questions   122
Form   123
Rhetorical Devices   123
Grammar and Sentence Structure   123
Parallel Structure   124
Wordiness   125
Writing   127

APPENDIX
Additional Model Passages   131
Rhetorical Checklist   138
Grammatical Checklist   139

INDEX OF RHETORICAL AND GRAMMATICAL TOPICS   141

TO THE STUDENT

Writing can be both educational and fun. It can be a way for you to tell about your life and personal experiences, to share your ideas about your studies, or to communicate to others what you have learned through reading. Sometimes you even learn what your own ideas are, or force yourself to form well-thought-out ideas and opinions, through writing. In the words of John Updike, "Writing and rewriting are a constant search for what one is saying."

Writing may not come easily to some of you. You may not have been asked to write much in the past, or you may not have been asked to write formal essays or to do the sort of "academic writing" that students are expected to do in college. This book is meant to be an introduction to that sort of writing. I have tried to present interesting model passages and writing assignments in order to make the learning as painless as possible. In fact, I hope you will enjoy sharing your experiences and ideas with your classmates and will come to feel, if you don't already, that writing is an enjoyable, challenging, creative activity, one that you do not just because "the teacher tells you to," but because you want to.

Part One
PARAGRAPHS

GROWING UP

ONE

A SPECIAL PLACE

Many children who live in the city see the country only in picture books or movies. Some kids, however, through the Fresh Air Fund (a program that sends city kids to the country), get to spend two weeks in the country every summer. In the following passage, Mario Puzo, who was a Fresh Air Fund kid, tells how the country was a special place for him.

from "Italians in Hell's Kitchen"
Mario Puzo

As a child I knew only the stone city. I had no conception of what the countryside could be. When I got to New Hampshire, when I ran barefoot along the dirt country roads, when I drove the cows home from pasture, when I darted° through fields of corn and waded through clear brooks, when I gathered warm brown speckled° eggs in the henhouse, when I drove a hay wagon drawn by two great horses — when I did all these things — I nearly went crazy with the joy of it. It was quite simply a fairy tale come true.

The family that took me in . . . gave me those magical times children never forget.* For two weeks every summer from the time I was nine to fifteen, I was happier than I have ever been before or since. The man was good with tools and built me a little playground with swings, sliding ponds°, seesaws. The woman had a beautiful flower and vegetable garden

moved very quickly
spotted

a smooth slope for children to slide down; a slide

---

*The three dots (. . .) mean that a part of the original text has been omitted.

the sound made by fat
when it is cooking

and let me pick from it. A cucumber or strawberry in the earth was a miracle. And then when they saw how much I loved picnics, the sizzling° frankfurters on a stick over the wood fire, the yellow roasted corn, they drove me out on Sunday afternoons to a lovely green grass mountainside. Only on Sundays it was never called a picnic; it was called "taking our lunch outside." . . .

There came a time, I was fifteen, when I was told I was too old to be sent away to the country as a Fresh Air Fund kid. It was the first real warning that I must enter the adult world, ready or not.

Comprehension Questions

1. Why did Puzo like the country so much?
2. What is the meaning of the expression "It was like a fairy tale come true"?
3. Why did Puzo have to stop going to the countryside?

Form

The passage is about what a special place the countryside was to Puzo ("I nearly went crazy with the joy of it"; "I was happier than I have ever been before or since"). In the passage, he gives many *details* (specific examples) of what he saw and did there. Following is an outline of the passage:

par. 1:   on what Puzo did in the countryside
details: — smelled grass and flowers and trees
           — ran barefoot
           — drove the cows home
             . . . etc.

par. 2:   on what the family did with Puzo
details: — man built a playground
           — woman let him pick from the garden
           — picnics

par. 3:   on when it ended

Rhetorical Devices

🗂 Puzo first mentions the "*stone* city," which contrasts with the soft, natural, colorful things described in the rest of the passage.

🗂 The repetition of *when*-clauses (clauses beginning with *when*) connects the first paragraph and makes it flow.

🗂 Puzo uses many *descriptive adjectives* (*dirt* country roads," "*warm brown speckled* eggs," "*sizzling* frankfurters," "*green grass* mountainside") which appeal to the reader's senses (seeing, feeling, smelling, hearing), and also *specific* rather than *general* verbs (*ran barefoot, darted, waded*) which tend to interest the reader and create visual images.

◻ Puzo suggests what a wonderful experience this was by using words related to magic: *fairy tale, magical times, a miracle.*

GRAMMAR AND SENTENCE STRUCTURE

Exercise 1: Sentence Ordering

Put the following sentences in the correct order.

1. The man was good with tools and built me a little playground with swings, sliding ponds, seesaws.
2. A cucumber or strawberry in the earth was a miracle.
3. And then when they saw how much I loved picnics, they drove me out on Sunday afternoons to a lovely green grass mountainside.
4. The woman had a beautiful flower and vegetable garden and let me pick from it.
5. Only on Sundays it was never called a picnic; it was called "taking our lunch outside."
6. The family that took me in gave me those magical times children never forget.

Exercise 2: Prepositions*

Fill in the correct prepositions (then check the passage at the beginning of this chapter).

_____ a child I knew only the stone city. I had no conception _____ what the countryside could be. When I got _____ New Hampshire, when I smelled grass and flowers and trees, when I ran barefoot _____ the dirt country roads, when I drove the cows home _____ pasture, when I darted _____ fields _____ corn and waded _____ clear brooks, when I gathered warm brown speckled eggs _____ the hen-house, when I drove a hay wagon drawn _____ two great horses — when I did all these things — I nearly went crazy _____ the joy _____ it.

Complete Sentences

Complete sentences in English include a *subject* (a noun or noun phrase) and a *predicate* (a verb followed by its object or *complement*). In the following sentences, the subject is underlined with one line and the predicate with two:

I	knew only the stone city.
It	was quite simply a fairy tale come true.
The family that took me in	gave me those magical times children never forget.

---

*May be omitted by basic writing students.

Exercise 3

In the following sentences, underline the subject with one line and the predicate with two.

1. I had no conception of what the countryside could be.
2. It was quite simply a fairy tale come true.
3. I was happier than I have ever been before or since.
4. The man was good with tools.
5. A cucumber or strawberry in the earth was a miracle.
6. They saw how much I loved picnics.
7. It was called "taking our lunch outside."
8. The stone city was my home.
9. The cows coming home from pasture were a lovely sight.
10. Fields of corn surrounded me.
11. A hay wagon drawn by two horses carried us out to the fields.
12. Those magical times will stay in my memory forever.

Sentence Fragments

Sometimes students incorrectly mark as a sentence (by starting with a capital letter and ending with a period) something which is not a complete sentence but is only a fragment:

INCORRECT:	Coney Island was a special place to me. When I was a child.
COMMENT:	"When I was a child" is a "dependent clause" (a group of words that has a subject and a verb but is not a complete sentence); it is really part of the preceding sentence.
CORRECT:	Coney Island was a special place to me when I was a child.
INCORRECT:	Walking around. You were surrounded by alluring colors and smells.
COMMENT:	"Walking around" has no subject and verb, and is therefore a fragment; it should be part of the following sentence.
CORRECT:	Walking around, you were surrounded by alluring colors and smells.
INCORRECT:	We would save our appetites for Nathan's. The best hot dog, french fries, and corn-on-the-cob stand in the world.
COMMENT:	"The best hot dog, french fries, and corn-on-the-cob stand in the world" has no subject and verb and is therefore not a sentence; it is part of the preceding sentence.
CORRECT:	We would save our appetites for Nathan's, the best hot dog, french fries, and corn-on-the-cob stand in the world.

Exercise 4

Correct the following sentence fragments.

1. When I knew we were going there. I would feel happy for weeks before the big event.
2. It was a long subway ride. To get there from the Bronx.
3. I hardly noticed it. Since I was so filled with excitement.
4. I didn't mind waiting in line a long time. For my turn to go on this great attraction.
5. When you got to the top of the giant ferris wheel, you could see all the rides. And the beach and ocean.
6. We wouldn't eat too much. Because we would save our appetites for Nathan's.
7. The hot dogs were extra long and delicious. The french fries thick, tasty, and cut in a special wrinkled way.
8. This made them look like no other french fries. Anywhere in the world.
9. Years later, as an adult. I came back to Coney Island.
10. I had no desire to go on those rides. Like the roller coaster that just make you dizzy. And give you an upset stomach.

Run-on Sentences

When someone writes two complete sentences with a comma between them, the result is a *run-on sentence.* (This error is also called a *comma splice.*)

INCORRECT:	The rides were great fun, the roller coaster is one of the biggest in the world.
COMMENT:	There are three main ways of correcting a run-on sentence:
	1. use a period (.)
	2. use a semicolon (;)
	3. use a connecting word like and, but, so, because, etc.
CORRECT:	The rides were great fun. The roller coaster is one of the biggest in the world.
OR:	The rides were fun; it has one of the biggest roller coasters in the world.
OR:	The rides were fun, and it has one of the biggest roller coasters in the world.

Another type of run-on sentence has no punctuation at all between two complete sentences. (The result is sometimes called a *fused sentence.*)

INCORRECT:	We would save our appetite for Nathan's the hot dogs were extra long and delicious, the french fries thick, tasty, and cut in a special wrinkled way.

CORRECT: We would save our appetites for Nathan's. The hot dogs were extra long
             and delicious, the french fries thick, tasty, and cut in a special wrinkled
             way.
             (OR use a semicolon, OR use the word <u>where</u> to connect the two sen-
             tences)

Exercise 5

Correct the following run-on sentences.

1. Coney Island was a special place to me when I was a child, my family didn't go
   there often but when I knew we were going, I would feel happy for weeks.
2. It was a long subway ride to get there from the Bronx, but I hardly noticed it the
   rides at Coney Island were great.
3. When you got to the top of the giant ferris wheel, you could see all the rides, walking around, you were surrounded by alluring colors and smells.
4. We wouldn't eat too much, because we would save our appetite for Nathan's, the
   hot dogs were extra long and delicious, the french fries thick, tasty, and cut in a
   special wrinkled way.
5. Years later, as an adult, I came back to Coney Island, it seemed crowded, dirty,
   and noisy.
6. I had no desire to go on those rides that make you dizzy, the french fries at
   Nathan's seemed greasy.
7. As a child I knew only the stone city, I had no conception of what the countryside
   could be.
8. I nearly went crazy with the joy of it, it was quite simply a fairy tale come true.
9. The family that took me in gave me those magical times children never forget,
   for two weeks every summer, I was happier than I have ever been before or since.
10. The man was good with tools and built me a little playground with swings, sliding
    ponds, seesaws, the woman had a beautiful flower and vegetable garden and let
    me pick from it.

Punctuation

Punctuation marks are important signals to your reader: they indicate where to pause,
where one sentence ends and another begins, where an extra thought has been put
into a sentence. Here are a few of the main rules of punctuation concerning commas,
semicolons, and colons.

1. **Use commas (,)**
   a. with a series of three or more words:
      The man was good with tools and built me a little playground with
      swings, sliding ponds, seesaws.

    b. between two descriptive adjectives:
> *I loved the thick, tasty french fries.*

    c. after a clause or long phrase placed at the beginning of a sentence:
> *When I got to New Hampshire, I nearly went crazy with the joy of it. Years later, as an adult, I came back to Coney Island.*

    d. before and after "extra" phrases or clauses that are put into the middle of a sentence (see "restrictive and nonrestrictive" on page 26):
> *Coney Island, a beach and amusement park area in Brooklyn, was a special place to me when I was a child.*

> *The Cyclone, which usually had a long line next to it, was one of the biggest roller coasters in the world.*

2. **Use semicolons (;)**

    a. to connect two related sentences:
> *As an adult, I came back to Coney Island; it seemed crowded, dirty, and noisy.*

    b. before "sentence connectors" (words like **moreover, nevertheless, therefore** — see page 16):
> *It was a long subway ride; nevertheless, I hardly noticed it.*

    c. in a series that already has commas in it:
> *I have three favorite places in New York: the Cloisters, where you can go for some peace and quiet; Central Park, a good place to go for concerts or plays; and the Brooklyn Botanic Garden, one of the cleanest and most beautiful places in the city.*

3. **Use colons (:)**

    a. after a complete sentence followed by a list:*
> *Walking around, you were surrounded by alluring colors and smells: pink cotton candy, giant cherry lollipops, and huge red jelly apples.*

    b. after a complete sentence followed by a word or phrase that explains or completes the idea of the sentence:*
> *There was one place I always looked forward to going to as a child: Coney Island.*

Exercise 6

Rewrite the following passage, putting in appropriate punctuation and capitalizing words at the beginning of sentences.

> *the family that took me in gave me those magical times children never forget for two weeks every summer from the time I was nine to fifteen I was happier than I have ever been before or since the man was good with tools and built me a little playground with swings sliding ponds seesaws the woman had a beautiful flower and vegetable garden and let me pick from it a cucumber or strawberry in the*

---

*A dash (—) can be used instead of a colon in these types of sentences.

earth was a miracle and then when they saw how much I loved picnics the siz-
zling frankfurters on a stick over the wood fire the yellow roasted corn they drove
me out on Sunday afternoons to a lovely green grass mountainside

Exercise 7: Proofreading

In the following paragraph, errors are underlined and the type of error is indicated in the margin. See the Grammatical Checklist on page 138 for the meaning of the correction symbols (punc. = punctuation, etc.). Rewrite the paragraph, correcting the indicated errors.

punc./punc.   Coney Island a beach and amusement park in Brooklyn was a special
          place to me when I was a child. My family didn't go that often, but when I
frag.   knew we were going there.* I would feel happy for weeks before the big
          event. It was a long subway trip to get there from the Bronx, but I hardly
frag./run-on noticed it. Since I was so filled with excitement. The rides were great fun, it
punc./punc. has one of the biggest roller coasters in the world the Cyclone and I didn't
          mind waiting in line a long time for my turn to go on this great attraction.

WRITING

Think of a place that was special to you when you were growing up (a place in the country, a park, a zoo, an amusement park, the circus, a lake, the ocean, etc.). List some specific things about the place that you liked, making an informal outline such as the following:

    Coney Island
      — rides (roller coaster, ferris wheel)
      — Nathan's (a food stand)

Tell one or more of your classmates about this place, then write a paragraph about it. You could begin by saying "_____ was a special place to me when I was a child." See the passage on page 131 as a model.

Proofreading

After writing your paragraph, proofread it, checking for the types of errors mentioned in the Grammatical Checklist on page 138. Be particularly careful to check for the types of errors that *you* have trouble with. (Your teacher will tell you which errors to look out for.)

---

*This arrow indicates that the fragment is *before* the indicated place; an arrow going in the opposite direction indicates that the fragment is *after* the indicated place.

TWO

A SPECIAL PERSON

Old people are often unappreciated in the United States. They have wisdom and experience that they could share with younger people, if younger people cared to ask. Many don't ask. Margaret Mead's family was an exception. In the following passage, Mead explains that her grandmother was an important person to her when she was growing up.

from *Blackberry Winter*
Margaret Mead

My paternal° grandmother, who lived with us from the time my parents married until she died in 1927 . . . , was the most decisive influence in my life. She sat at the center of our household. Her room—and my mother always saw to it that she had the best room, spacious and sunny, with a fireplace if possible—was the place to which we immediately went when we came in from playing or home from school. There my father went when he arrived in the house. There we did our lessons on the cherry-wood table with which she had begun housekeeping and which, later, was my dining room table for twenty-five years. There, sitting by the fire, erect° and intense, she listened to us and to all of Mother's friends and to our friends. In my early childhood she was also very active—cooking, preserving, growing flowers in the garden, and attentive to all the activities of the country and the farm, including the chickens that were always invading the lawn and that I was always being called from my book to shoo° away.

My mother was trustworthy in all matters that concerned our care.

on my father's side

straight, with good posture

chase

13

In ... in such a case

not serious

foolish, senseless

demand

Grandma was trustworthy in a quite different way. She meant exactly what she said, always. If you borrowed her scissors, you returned them. In like cases,° Mother would wail ineffectually, "Why does everyone borrow my scissors and never return them?" and Father would often utter idle° threats. But Grandma never threatened. She never raised her voice. She simply commanded respect and obedience by her complete expectation that she would be obeyed. And she never gave silly° orders. She became my model when, in later life, I tried to formulate a role for the modern parent who can no longer exact° obedience merely by virtue of being a parent and yet must be able to get obedience when it is necessary. Grandma never said, "Do this because Grandma says so," or "because Grandma wants you to do it." She simply said, "Do it," and I knew from her tone of voice that it was necessary.

Comprehension Questions

1. How was Mead's grandmother "the center of the household"?
2. How was Mead's mother different from her grandmother?
3. Why did Mead obey her grandmother?

Form

Mead is discussing how her grandmother was special to her ("the most decisive influence in my life").

    par. 1: on her grandmother's role in the house
             — everyone went to her room
             — they did their lessons there
             — she listened to everyone
             — she was active (cooking, preserving, etc.)
    par. 2: on how she commanded respect
             — meant what she said
             — unlike Mother and Father
             — never gave silly orders
             — a model for the modern parent

Rhetorical Devices

☐ Mead effectively uses *descriptive adjectives* in the passage ("the best room, *spacious* and *sunny*"; "the *cherry-wood* table"; "sitting by the fire, *erect* and *intense*"; etc.).

☐ Mead's descriptions come alive due to the use of *details* ("She was also very active—*cooking, preserving, growing flowers in the garden* . . . attentive to all the activities . . . , including the *chickens that were always invading the lawn*").

☐ Three sentences in paragraph 1 are connected by the repetition of *there* at the beginning ("*There* my father went . . . . *There* we did our lessons . . . . *There,* sitting by the fire . . . , she listened to us.").

☐ Mead explains how her grandmother commanded respect by contrasting her with her father and mother in paragraph 2.

GRAMMAR AND SENTENCE STRUCTURE

Exercise 1: Sentence Ordering

Put the following sentences in the correct order.

1. She meant exactly what she said, always.
2. In like case, Mother would wail ineffectually, "Why does everyone borrow my scissors and never return them?" and Father would often utter idle threats.
3. Grandma was trustworthy in a quite different way.
4. If you borrowed her scissors, you returned them.
5. But Grandma never threatened.
6. My mother was trustworthy in all matters that concerned our care.

Exercise 2: Prepositions*

Fill in the correct prepositions (then check the passage at the beginning of this chapter).

My paternal grandmother, who lived _____ us _____ the time my parents married until she died _____ 1927 was the most decisive influence _____ my life. She sat _____ the center _____ our household. Her room—and my mother saw _____ it that she had the best room, spacious and sunny, _____ a fireplace if possible—was the place _____ which we immediately went when we came _____ _____ playing or home _____ school.

Exercise 3: Punctuation

Rewrite the following passage, putting in appropriate punctuation and capitalizing words at the beginning of sentences.

she never raised her voice she simply commanded respect and obedience by her complete expectation that she would be obeyed and she never gave silly orders she became my model when in later life I tried to formulate a role for the modern parent who can no longer exact obedience merely by virtue of being a parent and yet must be able to get obedience when it is necessary Grandma never said do this because Grandma says so or because Grandma wants you to do it she simply said do it and I knew from her tone of voice that it was necessary.

Coordination

In order to have a good writing style, you should not write too many short, simple sentences. One way to avoid writing such sentences is to sometimes combine sentences by using the following words.

---

*May be omitted by basic writing students.

1. *and* **(to indicate addition of a related idea):**
   *She simply said, "Do it," **and** I knew from her tone of voice that it was necessary.*
2. *but* **(to indicate contrasting ideas):**
   *My family didn't go often, **but** when I knew we were going there, I would feel happy for weeks before the big event.*
3. *so* **(to indicate result):**
   *The biggest boy in the class liked Mary Ellen, **so** I fell in love with her too.*
4. *or* **(to indicate a choice):**
   *Maybe I fell in love with her because she was pretty, **or** maybe it was because she was quiet and shy, like me.*

Exercise 4

Combine the following sentences, using *and, but, so, or.*

1. Mother would wail, "Why does everyone always borrow my scissors and never return them?" Father would often utter idle threats.
2. The modern parent cannot demand obedience merely by virtue of being a parent. A parent must be able to get obedience when it is necessary.
3. We all greatly respected Grandma. We did what she told us to do.
4. I never actually met Mary Ellen on the street. I never did take her to parties.
5. Maybe I fell in love with her because she was pretty. Maybe it was because the biggest boy in the class liked her.
6. Mary Ellen was a special person to me. I'm not sure that I ever talked to her.
7. Puzo loved the countryside. He looked forward to going there every summer.
8. In the daytime he would run barefoot along country roads. He would dart through fields of corn and wade through clear brooks.
9. It was a long subway ride to get to Coney Island from the Bronx. I hardly noticed it, since I was so filled with excitement.
10. Coney Island had one of the biggest roller coasters in the world. I didn't mind waiting in line a long time for my turn to go on this great attraction.

Sentence Connectors

In addition to the words *and, but, so, or,* a number of other words can be used to connect sentences, indicating the following types of relations.

1. **Addition:**
   Nobody is interested in providing houses for the people of New York; **moreover,** *nobody is interested in providing jobs for the unemployed.* — adapted from Paul Goodman
   (other addition words: **furthermore, in addition, also, besides, besides that, additionally**)

2. Contrast:

In a great city, . . . hundreds of thousands have been ill housed, **yet** *we do not see science, industry, and labor enthusiastically enlisted in finding the quick solution to a definite problem.* — Paul Goodman

(other contrast words: **however, nevertheless, despite that, in spite of that, on the other hand, in contrast, nonetheless, still, on the contrary, even so, regardless of that)*

3. Result:

Industrialism demanded masses of workers ready and able to move . . . whenever necessary; **thus** *the extended family gradually shed its excess weight and the so-called "nuclear" family emerged.* — Alvin Toffler

(other result words: **therefore, consequently, hence, as a result, as a result of that, due to that, because of that, accordingly, for this reason, as a consequence, this being so)*

4. Time or order:

<u>*When they are near death, terminally ill patients*</u>* *begin to separate themselves from the interpersonal relationships in their environment;* **finally,** *they will require only one beloved person who can sit quietly and comfortably near.* — Elisabeth Kübler-Ross

(other time or order words: **first, second, third, first of all, next, then, subsequently, meanwhile, in the meantime, at last, afterward, later on, at the same time)*

5. Comparison:

Vehicles will always increase in direct proportion to the increase in spaces to hold them; **similarly,** *skyscrapers and boxlike apartment houses will increase as the money to build them increases.* — Eric Sevareid

(other comparison words: **likewise, in the same way, in the same manner)*

6. Illustration:

Simple knowledge of facts has its value. **For instance,** *to know who won the battle of Poltava . . . may win $64,000 for the possessor of this information.* — Carl R. Rogers

(other illustration words: **for example, as an example, as an illustration, to show what I mean, specifically)*

7. Explanation:

In real life . . . few women have much concern about <u>*heroes*</u>*;* **after all,** *there are few frontiers to conquer, or international spy rings to crack, or glorious wars to wage.* — Robert E. Gould

(other explanation words: **really, to tell the truth, when you think of it, in fact, as a matter of fact, actually, truly, in other words, that is, what I mean is)*

8. Emphasis:

<u>*A childless couple will prove more efficient navigating through job changes and geographic relocations;*</u> **indeed,** *anthropologist Margaret Mead has*

---

*The underlined words are not part of the original sentence.

pointed out that we may already be moving toward a system under which ... "parenthood would be limited to a smaller number of families whose principal function would be childrearing." — Alvin Toffler
*(other emphasis words: **in fact, as a matter of fact**)*

Exercise 5

Complete the following sentences.

1. Puzo enjoyed the freedom of the country; furthermore, . . .
2. Mead's grandmother didn't explain why Mead should obey her; nevertheless, . . .
3. Everyone in the family loved Mead's grandmother; therefore, . . .
4. When they went on picnics, the man cooked frankfurters over a wood fire; meanwhile, . . .
5. The subways in New York are terribly crowded; likewise, . . .
6. There are lots of interesting things to do in a big city; for example, . . .
7. Puzo enjoyed magical times in the country; in other words, . . .
8. Mead went to her grandmother's room as soon as she came into the house; in fact, . . .
9. Coney Island had great rides; for instance, . . .
10. From the top of the ferris wheel, you could see all the rides; besides that, . . .
11. I wanted to speak to Mary Ellen; however, . . .
12. Mary Ellen was the prettiest girl in the class; consequently, . . .

Subordination

When two sentences are combined in certain ways, one part is called the *main clause* and the other part is called the *dependent clause.* This type of combination, called *subordination,* occurs in sentences with the following types of relations between parts.

1. **Time:**
   ***When** I got to New Hampshire, . . . I nearly went crazy with the joy of it. —* Mario Puzo
   *(other time words: **before, after, until, as soon as, once, the moment, the instant, while, since, whenever, anytime, every time**)*
2. **Place:**
   *Puzo saw the beauties of nature **wherever** he looked.*
   *(other place words: **where, anywhere, everywhere**)*
3. **Reason:**
   *Grandma never said, "Do this **because** grandma says so." —* Margaret Mead
   *(other reason words: **since, for, as, inasmuch as**)*
4. **Purpose:**
   *Acres of houses and shops were demolished . . . **so that** great cathedrals could be built. —* Eric Sevareid
   *(another purpose expression: **in order that**)*

5. **Contrast:**
   Whereas *other kids seemed to look forward to Gym . . . , I dreaded the thought of sports.* — Peter Candell
   (other contrast words: **although, even though, though, while, where, even if, no matter if)**

6. **Result:**
   American society has tried **so** *hard . . . to defend the practice and theory of production for profit and not primarily for use* **that** *now it has [made] its jobs profitable and useless.* — Paul Goodman
   Gym was **such** *an unpleasant experience* **that** *I sometimes pretended to be sick in order to miss it.*
   (In this type of sentence, **so** *is used before adjectives and* **such** *before nouns.)*

7. **Manner:**
   Margaret Mead has pointed out that we may already be moving toward a system under which, **as** *she puts it, "parenthood would be limited to a smaller number of families. . . ."* — Alvin Toffler
   (other manner words: **as if, as though)**

8. **Comparison:**
   I think he tells her a great deal **more than** *he tells us.* — E.B. White
   He was **as** *careless of material things* **as** *he had always been.* — Margaret Mead
   (other comparison expressions: **less . . . than, the most, the least)**

9. **Condition:**
   If you borrowed her scissors, you returned them. — Margaret Mead
   (other condition words: **unless, whether or not, as long as, provided that)**

Exercise 6

Complete the following sentences.

1. Puzo felt sad after . . .
2. Margaret Mead liked to go wherever . . .
3. Many people live in big cities because . . .
4. Puzo's family sent him to the country every summer so that . . .
5. Many people move to New York City, although . . .
6. Puzo enjoyed the country so much that . . .
7. Mead's grandmother spoke to her grandchildren as if . . .
8. Puzo was less happy in the city than . . .
9. New York City is a good place to live if . . .
10. I liked Coney Island because . . .
11. As a child, I felt happy when . . .
12. I never talked to Mary Ellen, although . . .

Exercise 7

Rewrite sentences 1, 2, 3, 5, 9, 10, and 12 from Exercise 6, moving the dependent clause to the front of the sentence. For example, instead of "Puzo felt sad after he came home from the country," you should write "After he came home from the country, Puzo felt sad."

Exercise 8: Proofreading

In the following paragraph, errors are underlined and the type of error is indicated in the margin. Rewrite the paragraph, correcting the indicated errors.

comb.*	I was in the fourth grade. Mary Ellen Fischer was a special person to me.
comb.	This may seem strange. I'm not sure I ever talked to her. What was special was that I was in love with her. I'm not sure what it was about her that made
run-on	me fall in love with her, she was, I think, the prettiest girl in my class. She was
frag.	rather quiet and shy. Like me. Maybe it was that the biggest boy in the
punc./punc.	class Marty Warner (who was also the best athlete) liked Mary Ellen. For whatever reason, I loved Mary Ellen.

WRITING

Think of a person who was special to you when you were growing up (your father, mother, sister, brother, aunt, uncle, cousin, a good friend, a neighbor, a boyfriend or girlfriend, etc.). List some things you liked about this person, making an informal outline such as the following:

> Mary Ellen Fischer
> — I "loved" her (in the fourth grade)
> — pretty
> — quiet and shy
> — I daydreamed about taking her to parties

Tell one or more of your classmates about this person, then write a paragraph about him or her. The paragraph could begin "_____ was a special person to me when I was a child." See the passage on page 131 as a model.

Proofreading

After writing your paragraph, proofread it, particularly checking for the types of errors that *you* have trouble with.

---

*Make these two sentences into one sentence by using a connecting word.

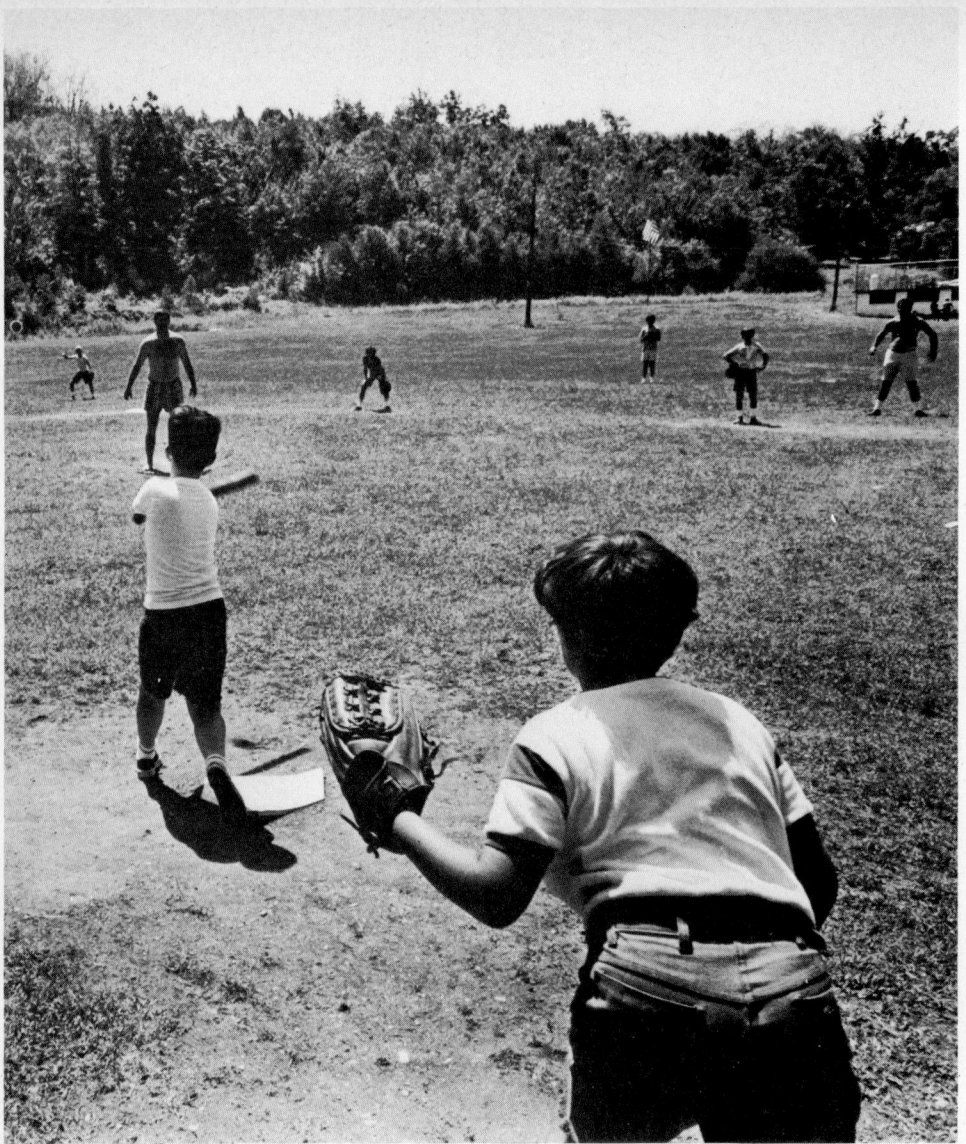

THREE

A MEMORABLE EXPERIENCE

There are some memorable experiences that you wouldn't mind forgetting. That's the type described by Peter Candell in the following passage. Boys spend a lot of time playing sports in the United States. But what happens to the boys who aren't good in sports? Read on.

from "Out in Right Field"
Peter Candell

Throughout my entire school career, the time of day I dreaded° most was Gym class. Whereas other kids seemed to look forward to Gym as some sort of relief from sitting at a desk and listening to a teacher, I dreaded the thought of sports.

The curse° followed me throughout my entire life. In elementary school, part of the year we played baseball outdoors. The two best players (never me) were captains and they chose—one by one—players for their teams. The choosing went on and on, the better players getting picked first and me and my type last.

During the game I always played the outfield. Right field. Far right field. And there I would stand in the hot sun wishing I was anyplace else in the world. Every so often° a ball looked like it was coming in my direction and I prayed to god that it wouldn't happen. If it did come, I promised god to be good for the next thirty-seven years if he let me catch it—especially if it was a fly ball. The same thing occurred when it was my turn to bat. It was bad enough, but if there were any runners on base—or any outs—and it all depended on me—I knew we were lost.

dreaded°	didn't want to happen
curse°	evil magic spell
Every so often°	**Every** . . . from time to time

23

Comprehension Questions

1. What do students do in Gym class?
2. Why wasn't Candell ever a captain?
3. How did Candell feel when he saw a ball coming?

Form

Candell is telling how he felt about sports as an elementary school student.

> par. 1: how he dreaded sports
> par. 2: on choosing teams (Candell was picked last)
> par. 3: played right field
>   — wished he were somewhere else
>   — prayed that a ball wouldn't come
>   — felt the same when he came to bat

Rhetorical Devices

☐ Candell stresses what a terrible experience this was for him by using the negative word *dreaded,* and by explaining that he *prayed to god* that a ball wouldn't come.

☐ He emphasizes his isolation by contrasting the good players and himself (*other kids/I, the two best players/never me, the better players/me and my type*).

☐ Baseball players know that one is not very likely to get a ball in right field. Candell stressed that this was his position through *repetition* ("Right field. Far right field").

☐ The expression *whereas* is used to indicate contrast ("*Whereas* other kids seemed to look forward to Gym, I dreaded the thought of sports"). Other expressions of contrast are *although* and *even though.*

GRAMMAR AND SENTENCE STRUCTURE

Exercise 1: Sentence Ordering

Put the following sentences in the correct order.

1. The two best players (never me) were captains and they chose—one by one—players for their teams.
2. And there I would stand in the hot sun wishing I was anyplace else in the world.
3. During the game I always played the outfield.
4. In elementary school, part of the year we played baseball outdoors.

5. The choosing went on and on, the better players getting picked first and me and
my type last.

Exercise 2: Prepositions*

Fill in the correct prepositions (then check the passage at the beginning of this
chapter).

_____ my entire school career, the time _____ day I dreaded most was Gym
class. Whereas other kids seemed to look forward _____ Gym as some sort
_____ relief _____ sitting _____ a desk and listening _____ a teacher, I
dreaded the thought _____ sports.

Exercise 3: Punctuation

Rewrite the following passage, putting in appropriate punctuation and capitalizing
words at the beginning of sentences.

*during the game I always played the outfield and there I would stand in the
hot sun wishing I was anyplace else in the world every so often a ball looked like
it was coming in my direction and I prayed to god that it wouldn't happen if it did
come I promised god to be good for the next thirty-seven years if he let me catch it
especially if it was a fly ball*

Adjective Clauses

Sentences in English often include *adjective clauses* (clauses describing a noun)
which begin with the words *who, whom, which, that, whose, where,* or *when*:

> *In my psychiatric practice I have seen a number of male patients ... **who have
> equated moneymaking with a sense of masculinity.*** — Robert E. Gould

> *The patients **whom I spoke to** felt insecure about their masculinity.* — Robert E.
> Gould

> *Her room ... was the place **to which we immediately went** when we came in
> from playing or home from school.* — Margaret Mead

> *The family **that took me in** gave me those magical times children never forget.*
> — Mario Puzo

> *I'd almost forgotten about Miss Wooley, **whose name and image now came
> raging back without hesitation.*** — John A. Williams

> *I have an increasing admiration for the teacher in the country school **where we
> have a third-grade scholar in attendance.*** — E. B. White

> *There came a time ... **when I was told I was too old to be sent away to the
> country as a Fresh Air Fund kid.*** — Mario Puzo

---

*May be omitted by basic writing students.

Restrictive and Nonrestrictive Clauses

When a clause tells which person or thing is being discussed, it is called a *restrictive clause*; when a clause does not identify a person or thing but only gives additional information, it is *nonrestrictive*:

1. **Restrictive clauses:**

    *They gave me those magical times **that children never forget.*** — Mario Puzo

    *The time of day **that I dreaded most** was Gym class.* — Peter Candell

    *Unfortunately, the number of technologists **who know how to set off the destruct system** has increased.* — Donald Morris

    (If the clauses set in bold type are omitted, the sentences are unclear; we don't know which thing or person is being discussed. Notice that we use no commas with this type of clause.)

2. **Nonrestrictive clauses:**

    *The most fundamental kind of love, **which underlies all types of love,** is brotherly love.* — Erich Fromm

    *As the furnace had an automatic fire arrangement, the principal hazards were to himself and not to the neighbors, **in whose children he was deeply interested.*** — Margaret Mead

    *When summer school was over, his club, **which he had founded and in which he ate lunch every day,** closed.* — Margaret Mead

    (The clauses set in bold type can be omitted without making the meaning of the sentences unclear. Notice that we use commas before and after this type of clause; also, we do not use the connecting word that in this type of clause.)

Exercise 4

Combine the following sentences by making one into an adjective clause.

1. The man was good with tools. Puzo visited the man every summer. (use *whom*)
2. Puzo lived in the city. Puzo had the opportunity of visiting the country every summer. (use *who*)
3. The farm had fields of corn. Puzo stayed at the farm. (use *where*)
4. The time came. Puzo could no longer go to the country as a Fresh Air kid at this time. (use *when*)
5. Mead's grandmother lived with the family from the time Margaret's parents married. Mead's grandmother was a decisive influence in Margaret's life. (use *who*)
6. Her grandmother's room was spacious and sunny. Her grandmother's room was the best room in the house. (use *which*)
7. Margaret had a girlfriend. The girlfriend's father was a writer. (use *whose*)
8. Candell disliked one class most. The class was Gym class. (use *that*)

9. Candell dreaded Gym class. At this time, he always felt foolish. (use *when*)
10. Candell was picked last. Candell was not a very good player. (use *who*)

Omitting the Connecting Word

When the connecting word in a restrictive clause is followed by a *subject* and a *verb,* it can be omitted:

The patients whom *I*   *spoke to* felt insecure.
                (subject)   (verb)

Connector omitted:

The patients I spoke to felt insecure.

Exercise 5

Rewrite the following sentences, omitting the connecting word at the beginning of the adjective clause.

1. The fields of corn that Puzo darted through seemed like something out of a fairy tale to him.
2. The family gave him those magical times that children never forget.
3. The man whom Puzo lived with built him a little playground.
4. The person whom Margaret admired most was her grandmother.
5. The room which Margaret went to upon entering the house was her grandmother's.
6. One place where the grandmother enjoyed working was in the garden.
7. The time of day which Candell dreaded most was Gym class.
8. Candell especially hated the part of year when they played baseball outdoors.

Appositives

An "appositive" is like an adjective clause, but it is a phrase rather than a clause (it does not have a subject and a verb):

> *The extended family gradually shed its excess weight and the "nuclear" family emerged,* . . . **a portable family unit consisting only of parents and a small set of children.** — Alvin Toffler

> *Super-industrialism, the* **next stage of eco-technological development,** *requires even higher mobility.* — Alvin Toffler

Exercise 6

Combine the following sentences by making one into an appositive phrase.

1. Puzo was a city child. Puzo had no conception of what the countryside could be.

2. The man and woman were a kind couple. They took Puzo on picnics every Sunday.

3. Mead loved her grandmother. Her grandmother was an intelligent, intense woman.

4. Mead spent a lot of time in her grandmother's room. Her grandmother's room was the best room in the house.

5. Mead's grandmother was active around the house. She was attentive to all the activities of the country and the farm.

6. Mead's grandmother was respected in a special way. She always expected everyone to obey her orders.

7. Gym was a relief from sitting at a desk for some kids. Gym was an experience that Candell dreaded.

8. Candell was one of the worst ballplayers. Candell was always one of the last boys to be picked by the captains.

Exercise 7: Proofreading

In the following paragraph, errors are underlined and the type of error is indicated in the margin. Rewrite the paragraph, correcting the indicated errors.

comb./run-on   I was 16 years old. I got a learner's permit to learn how to drive, I got the permit just before my family was going to the country for our summer

comb.   vacation. I started practicing on country roads. It should have been easy.

run-on   There wasn't much traffic on those quiet country roads one thing that wasn't easy about it was that my father proved to be a very nervous teach-

frag.   er. Having himself learned to drive at a rather old age, and being himself quite ill-at-ease behind the wheel. "Don't go so fast!" "You're over too much to the left!" "You're over too much to the right!" Despite this, I was finally ready to take my driving test.

WRITING

Think of an experience you had while you were growing up. It can be a pleasant or an unpleasant experience (although often, unpleasant, embarassing, or frightening experiences make the best stories). Make an informal outline of the experience (When did it happen? Where? Why were you there? What happened? What was the result?). The following is an outline of the experience described on page 131.

> Learning to drive
> — was 16 years old
> — practiced with my father in the country
> — failed first test
> — finally passed
> — first driving experiences

Tell one or more of your classmates about the experience, then write about it. See the passage on page 131 as a model.

Proofreading

After writing your paragraph, proofread it, particularly checking for the types of errors that *you* have trouble with.

EDUCATION

FOUR

MEMORABLE TEACHERS

Much of our growing-up time is spent in classrooms. This time can be wonderfully well-spent or a painful waste of time. A lot depends on the teacher. Following are descriptions of two teachers who made a difference, one way or the other.

from "Time and Tide"
John A. Williams

I'd almost forgotten about Miss Wooley, whose name and image now came raging° back without hesitation. She taught arithmetic. If you looked like you were going to make an error, she'd let you have it° with anything handy—fists, an eraser, a ruler. Because of Miss Wooley, I make my eights from the wrong side. I know that it's easy to place psychological blame on the past, but the truth of the matter is that Miss Wooley scared me and ruined my capacity forever to deal effectively with numbers. That I do remember her and have written about her speaks for itself;° Miss Wooley was one of those experiences I could not outgrow.

from "Education"
E. B. White

I have an increasing admiration for the teacher in the country school where we have a third-grade scholar in attendance. She not only undertakes° to instruct her charges in all the subjects of the first three grades, but she manages to function quietly and effectively as a guardian of their health, their clothes, their habits, their mothers, and their snowball engagements.

(margin notes)
raging° — rushing (with anger)
let ... have it° — **let** ... hit you
speaks for itself° — **speaks** ... shows that this is true
undertakes° — tries

| terribly difficult | She has been doing this sort of Augean° task for twenty years, and is both |

terribly difficult | She has been doing this sort of Augean° task for twenty years, and is both
kind and wise. She cooks for the children on the stove that heats the room,
cool . . . make them | and she can cool their passions° or warm their soup with equal compe-
calm when they are | tence. She conceives their costumes, cleans up their messes, and shares
upset | their confidences. My boy already regards his teacher as his great friend,
and I think tells her a great deal more than he tells us.

Comprehension Questions

1. What does Williams remember most about Miss Wooley?
2. How did Miss Wooley deal with errors?
3. Why does White admire his child's teacher?
4. What shows that White's child feels that his teacher is his friend?

Form

Many paragraphs include a sentence that states the main idea of the paragraph. Such a sentence is called a *topic sentence*. The topic sentence of the first paragraph is "Miss Wooley scared me and ruined my capacity forever to deal effectively with numbers." The topic sentence of the second paragraph is the first sentence: "I have an increasing admiration for the teacher in the country school where we have a third-grade scholar in attendance." Often, the first sentence of a paragraph is the topic sentence. The first paragraph may be outlined as follows:

main idea: Miss Wooley scared me and ruined my capacity to
             deal with numbers.

details: — She taught arithmetic
             — She "let you have it" for errors
             — make my eights from the wrong side
             — couldn't outgrow her

Notice that the details *support* or *explain* the main idea. The second paragraph may be outlined as follows:

main idea: I have an increasing admiration for my child's
             teacher.

details: — instructs students in all the subjects
             — a guardian of their health
             — kind and wise
             — cooks
               . . . etc.

Rhetorical Devices

First paragraph:

◻ Williams communicates his anger by using the strong negative word *raging* in the first sentence.

◪   He creates a visual image with specific details ("She'd let you have it with . . . *fists, an eraser, a ruler*").

◪   The expression *because of* indicates a causal relationship ("*Because of* Miss Wooley, I make my eights from the wrong side"). Other causal expressions are *due to* and *as a result of.*

Second paragraph:

◪   White emphasizes the teacher's concern for all aspects of the students' lives by repeating the word *their* ("*their* health, *their* clothes, *their* habits, *their* mothers, and *their* snowball engagements").

◪   He achieves a pleasant effect by repeating the "hard *c*" sound ("She *c*onceives their *c*ostumes, *c*leans up their messes, and shares their *c*onfidences").

◪   He connects his ideas with the paired or "correlative" conjunctions *not only . . . but* ("She *not only* undertakes to instruct her charges . . . , *but* she manages to . . .") and also uses *both . . . and* ("She is *both* kind *and* wise"). Other correlative conjunctions are *either . . . or* (You can be *either* in Mr. Brown's class *or* in Mr. Smith's) and *neither . . . nor* (*Neither* John *nor* Bill is coming to school today).

GRAMMAR AND SENTENCE STRUCTURE

Exercise 1: Sentence Ordering

Put the following sentences in the correct order.

1. If you looked like you were going to make an error, she'd let you have it with anything handy — fists, an eraser, a ruler.

2. I know that it's easy to place psychological blame on the past, but the truth of the matter is that Miss Wooley scared me and ruined my capacity forever to deal effectively with numbers.

3. Because of Miss Wooley, I make my eights from the wrong side.

4. She taught arithmetic.

5. I'd almost forgotten about Miss Wooley, whose name and image now came raging back without hesitation.

Exercise 2: Prepositions*

Fill in the correct prepositions (then check the passage at the beginning of this chapter).

I have an increasing admiration _____ the teacher _____ the country school where we have a third-grade scholar _____ attendance. She not only undertakes to instruct her charges _____ all the subjects _____ the first three grades, but she

---

*May be omitted by basic writing students.

manages to function quietly and effectively _____ a guardian _____ their health, their clothes, their habits, their mothers, and their snowball engagements. She has been doing this sort _____ Augean task _____ twenty years, and is both kind and wise.

Exercise 3: Punctuation

Rewrite the following passage, putting in appropriate punctuation and capitalizing words at the beginning of sentences.

I'd almost forgotten about Miss Wooley whose name and image now came raging back without hesitation she taught arithmetic if you looked like you were going to make an error she'd let you have it with anything handy fists an eraser a ruler because of Miss Wooley I make my eights from the wrong side

Subject-Verb Agreement Review

In English, verbs in the present tense and also the verb *be* in the past tense must *agree* with their subject (both must be singular or both must be plural):

singular	plural
William's teacher **is** mean.	His teachers **are** mean.
She **punishes** the children.	They **punish** the children.
Puzo **was** happy in the country.	Puzo's friends **were** happy in the city.
The country teacher **does** a lot of work.	Country teachers **do** a lot of work.
The country teacher **has** a hard time.	Country teachers **have** a hard time.

The *singular* verb form is used with the "third-person singular" subjects *he, she, it, Bill, Jane, the car,* etc.; the *plural* verb form is used with other subjects: *I, you, we, they.* An exception to this rule is that the singular past form *was* is used with *I.*

Exercise 4

Rewrite the following paragraph, beginning with the plural form "Country teachers." The first sentence will begin "Country teachers not only undertake to instruct their charges in . . . ."

The country teacher not only undertakes to instruct her charges in all the subjects of the first three grades, but she manages to function quietly and effectively as a guardian of their health, their clothes, their habits, their mothers, and their snowball engagements. She has been doing this sort of Augean task for twenty years, and is both kind and wise. She cooks for the children on the stove that heats the room, and she can cool their passions or warm their soup with equal competence. She conceives the students' costumes, cleans up their messes, and shares their confidences.

Exercise 5

Rewrite the following paragraph, beginning with the singular form "My English teacher." The first sentence will be "My English teacher seems great to me."

My English teachers seem great to me. It's hard to say exactly what's greatest about them. One thing is their love of words. They love to talk themselves, and appreciate it when students use words well. Also, they love books. In our classes, we don't use textbooks; we use paperback books. The teachers like to discuss the books and they have us write reports and essays on what we have read. They don't correct every mistake in our essays. They write comments on the essays showing that they have read them carefully and tried to understand them. They don't just tell us what's wrong with them, but also what's right.

Exercise 6

Speak to a fellow classmate about what he/she likes to do in his/her free time and why he/she likes to do this. Then write a paragraph in the present tense about what your classmate does. You will have to use the "final s" on many of the verbs. (For students who need extra practice: Do exercise 6 with one or more members of your family, with friends, etc. Keep on doing it, once a week, until you no longer make "s-form" errors.)

Subject-Verb Agreement: Special Problems

Be careful to follow these special rules of subject-verb agreement:

1. Singular subjects joined by *and* are generally plural:
    *White **and** his wife **like** their son's teacher.*
2. After a subject joined by *either . . . or, neither . . . nor,* or *not only . . . but also,* the verb agrees with the nearest part of the subject:
    *Neither Williams' friends nor **Williams wants** to see Miss Wooley again.*
3. Indefinite pronouns (*someone, anyone, no one, everyone, somebody, anybody, nobody, everybody, one, each, either, neither*) usually take singular verbs:
    *No one **was** allowed to make a mistake in Miss Wooley's class.*
4. "Quantity words" (*some, none, any, all, part, half, enough, a lot, most*) can be singular or plural, depending on the noun that follows:
    *Some of the **cows were** sick.*
    *Some of the **grass was** dry.*

5. A noun referring to a group (*family, class, group, committee, jury, faculty, team, crowd*) is usually singular, but can be plural if referring to individual members separately:

    *My family **is** living in New York.*

    *My family **are** going to different places for their summer vacation this year.*

6. *There is* and *there are* agree with the following noun:

    *There is a lot of **work** to do in this class.*

    *There are a lot of **books** to read.*

7. A verb phrase used as a subject is singular:

    ***Driving the cows home was** great fun for Puzo.*

8. Verbs agree with their subjects, not with the objects of prepositions following the subjects:

    *A **herd** of cows **was** hard to drive.*

9. A phrase that appears between a subject and a verb does not affect the verb:

    ***White's son,** as well as all the other students, **loves** his schoolteacher.*

10. The subject of a verb sometimes appears before a connecting word such as *who, which, that*:

    *The **students** who **do** the work will get good grades.*

    *The **books** that **are** in that box are for the class.*

Exercise 7

Choose the correct verb in the following sentences.

1. Not only the students but also the teacher (is/are) interested in this subject.
2. The class (has/have) a test every Friday.
3. The fields of corn (looks/look) beautiful this morning.
4. The woman who (teaches/teach) White's son is interested in her students.
5. The man and woman (was/were) happy to have Puzo stay with them.
6. Everybody (needs/need) a good education.
7. There (was/were) some fresh strawberries in the garden.
8. Some of the corn (is/are) ready to eat.
9. Mary, unlike her brothers, (does/do) all her schoolwork.

Pronoun Agreement

Like verbs, pronouns must agree with the noun to which they refer, sometimes called *antecedent* (*Puzo* loved the country. *He* went there every summer). Be careful to follow these special rules of pronoun agreement:

1. Indefinite pronouns (see above, rule 3) are followed by singular pronouns:

    ***Everybody** can read whatever book **he wants** to.*

2. A pronoun following *either . . . or, neither . . . nor,* or *not only . . . but also* agrees with the nearest noun:

   *Either the students or **the teacher** must express **his** opinion.*

3. A group noun (see above, rule 5) usually takes a singular pronoun, but can take a plural pronoun if individual members are considered separately:

   *The class is taking **its** test.*

   *The class are raising **their** hands.*

Exercise 8

Choose the correct verb and pronoun in the following sentences.

1. Everyone (does/do) (his/their) job on a farm.
2. All the Fresh Air kids (were/was) looking forward to (their/his) vacation.
3. A person who (don't/doesn't) play ball well usually dislikes (their/his) Gym class.
4. Every student in Miss Wooley's class (were/was) afraid to raise (their/his) hand.
5. Either John or his friend Bill (has/have) to speak to (his/their) father.
6. The class (was/were) eager to go on (its/their) trip.
7. Each student (is/are) anxious about (his/their) mark on the test.
8. Not only the students but also the teacher (is/are) happy about (his/their) vacation.

Pronoun Reference

Pronouns (words like *he, she, it, they, this, that*) must clearly refer to a particular noun or phrase. Avoid the following errors in pronoun reference:

1. **ambiguous reference** (the pronoun could refer to either one of two people or things):

INCORRECT:	John told Bill that he was a good student.
COMMENT:	Who was a good student, John or Bill?
CORRECT:	John said, "Bill, you are a good student."
OR:	John said that Bill was a good student.
OR:	John told Bill that Bill was a good student.

2. **remote reference** (the preceding noun is too far away from the pronoun):

INCORRECT:	I put the textbooks on my desk, then ate lunch and listened to music for a while. I planned to look at them later.
COMMENT:	What does them refer to?
CORRECT:	I put the textbooks on my desk, then ate lunch and listened to music for a while. I planned to look at the textbooks later.

3. no referent:

> INCORRECT: Teaching is a very satisfying profession. <u>This</u> is my ambition.
>
> COMMENT: What does <u>this</u> refer to?
>
> CORRECT: Teaching is a very satisfying profession. To become a teacher is my ambition.

4. vague use of *they*:

> INCORRECT: There are a lot of crimes in New York. <u>They</u> ought to do something about it.
>
> COMMENT: Who is <u>they</u>?
>
> CORRECT: There are a lot of crimes in New York. The city government (or "the police" or "the people of the city") ought to do something about it.

Exercise 9

Rewrite the following sentences, correcting the errors in pronoun reference.

1. High school classes in New York are crowded and they haven't done much to improve the situation.
2. Mary told Jane that she had to study for her test.
3. Students learn a lot from their teachers. It helps them to become responsible adults.
4. Cars cause a lot of pollution. If they were fined, they would make better cars.
5. I bought a new notebook, then went to the bakery and did some grocery shopping. When I got home, I couldn't find it.
6. The subways in New York are dirty and it is expensive.
7. Jack told Jim that his teacher wanted to see him.
8. The salaries in that school are low. Many of them would rather work somewhere else.

Exercise 10: Proofreading

In the following paragraphs, errors are *not* underlined, but are indicated in the margin. Find the errors; then rewrite the paragraph, correcting the errors.

punc.	I'll always remember Mr. Shaw my best high school English teacher, one
run-on/punc.	of the greatest writers of all time is a Shaw George Bernard Shaw. My high
v.sg.*	school teacher weren't George Bernard Shaw, but he still seemed great to
run-on	me, at least as great as George Bernard Shaw it's hard to say exactly what
	was greatest about him. One thing was his love of words. He loved to talk
comb.	himself. He appreciated it when students used words well. I remember him
v.pl.	saying, "Try to use words that produces an image, like 'copper pennies on

---

*"V. sing." means a singular verb form should be used on this line; a plural verb form is incorrectly used here.

a white, marble table.'" Those copper pennies may not have been the
v.pl./frag. greatest image in the world, but they has stayed with me to this day. And
challenged me to do as well or better in my own use of words.

WRITING

Think of a particularly good teacher or class, or a particularly bad teacher or class.
Make an informal outline of some of the things you liked or disliked about this teacher
or class, such as the following:

Mr. Shaw (my English teacher)
— loved words
— loved books
— we read paperbacks
— he had an "air of mystery"

Tell one or more of your classmates about the teacher or class, then write about it.
Make the first sentence of the paragraph your topic sentence. (It could be "_____
was one of the best teachers I have ever had in my life.") See the paragraph on page
132 as a model.

Proofreading

After writing your paragraph, proofread it, particularly checking for the types of errors
that *you* have trouble with.

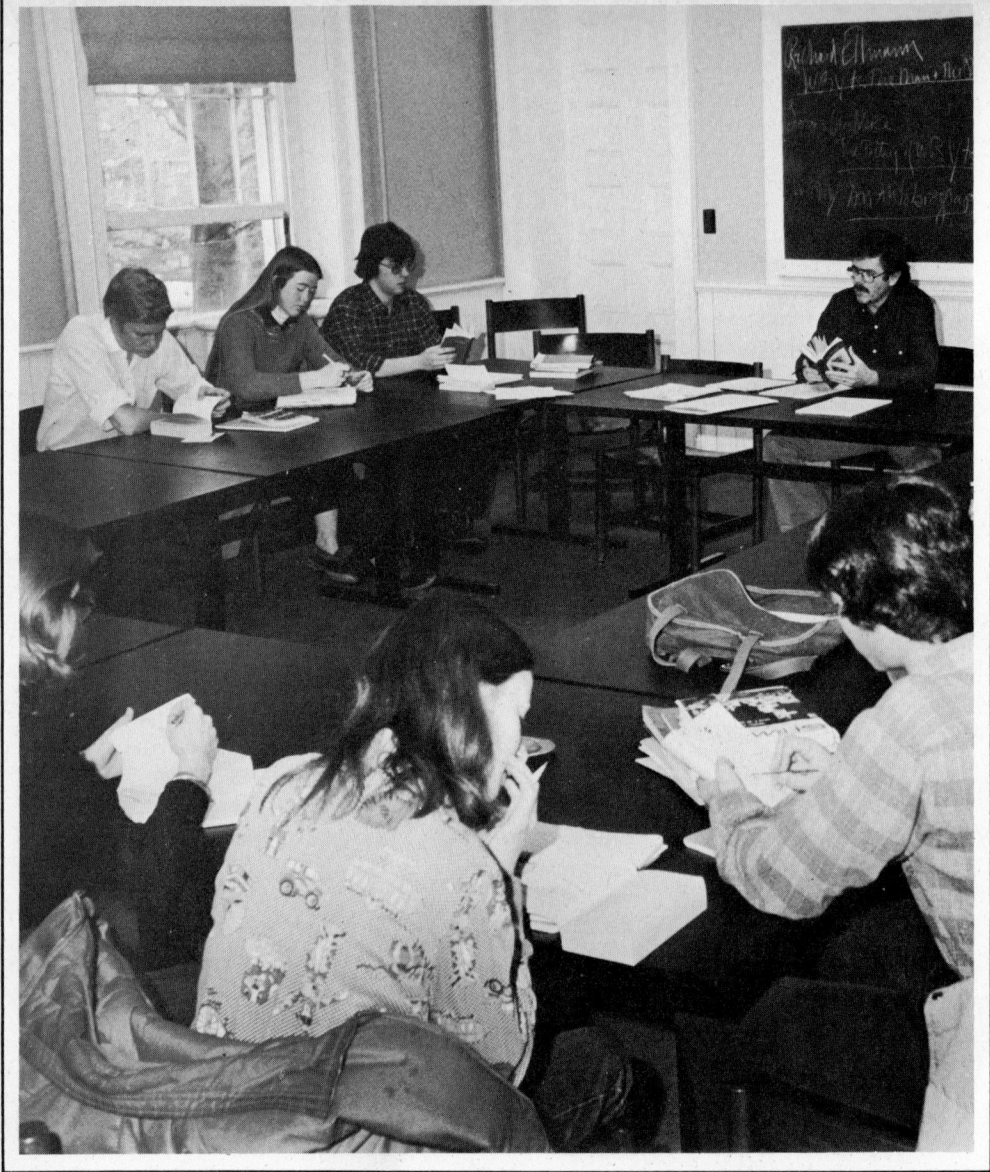

FIVE

THE PURPOSE OF EDUCATION

Perhaps you have sometimes asked yourself, when sitting in a classroom, "Why am I here?" or "What am I getting out of this?" Unfortunately, the answers to these two questions might sometimes have been "No good reason!" and "Nothing!" In the following passage, Carl Rogers offers a guideline on what can make classes more useful.

from *On Becoming a Person*
Carl R. Rogers

I believe I am accurate in saying that educators too are interested in learnings which make a difference. Simple knowledge of facts has its value. To know who won the battle of Poltava, or when the umpteenth° opus of Mozart was first performed, may win $64,000 or some other sum for the possessor of this information, but I believe educators in general are a little embarrassed by the assumption that the acquisition of such knowledge constitutes education. Speaking of this reminds me of a forceful statement made by a professor of agronomy° in my freshman year in college. Whatever knowledge I gained in his course has departed completely, but I remember how, with World War I as his background, he was comparing factual knowledge with ammunition.° He wound up his little discourse with the exhortation,° "Don't be a damned ammunition wagon; be a rifle!" I believe most educators would share this sentiment that knowledge exists primarily for use.

any large number

study of how to grow plants for food

bullets used for guns
strong advice

43

Comprehension Questions

1. What is more important than simple knowledge of facts?
2. When the umpteenth opus of Mozart was first performed is an example of what?
3. What did Rogers' professor mean when he said, "Don't be a damned ammunition wagon; be a rifle!"

Form

Rogers is expressing the opinion that what students learn in school should be useful to them. The paragraph could be outlined as follows:

main idea:	Learning should make a difference.
details:	— facts have some value
	— learning facts isn't education
	— a short anecdote supporting the main idea
concluding sent.:	Knowledge exists primarily for use.
	(repeating the main idea)

Rhetorical Devices

☐ Rogers emphasizes the lack of importance of facts by using the word *simple* and by giving a not very important use for facts (winning money on a quiz show like "The $64,000 Question").

☐ Rogers supports his point by using an interesting quote from an authority (a college professor).

☐ The word *but* indicates contrast ("To know who won . . . may win $64,000, *but* I believe educators in general are a little embarrassed . . ."). Other expressions of contrast are *nevertheless, however, despite that, in spite of that.*

☐ Rogers uses the expression *in general* to make a general statement, or generalization ("Educators *in general* are a little embarrassed by the assumption that the acquisition of such knowledge constitutes education"). Other generalizing expressions are *generally, generally speaking, on the whole, as a rule,* and quantity expressions like *most* (*most* educators . . ."), *many, the majority of, all, almost all, a large number of,* etc.

GRAMMAR AND SENTENCE STRUCTURE

Exercise 1: Sentence Ordering

Put the following sentences in the correct order.

1. He wound up his little discourse with the exhortation, "Don't be a damned ammunition wagon; be a rifle!"

2. Speaking of this reminds me of a forceful statement made by a professor of agronomy in my freshman year in college.

3. I believe most educators would share this sentiment that knowledge exists primarily for use.

4. To know who won the battle of Poltava may win $64,000 for the possessor of this information, but I believe educators in general are a little embarrassed by the assumption that the acquisition of such knowledge constitutes education.

5. Whatever knowledge I gained in his course has departed completely, but I remember how, with World War I as his background, he was comparing factual knowledge with ammunition.

Exercise 2: Prepositions*

Fill in the correct prepositions (then check the passage at the beginning of this chapter).

I believe I am accurate _____ saying that educators too are interested _____ learnings which make a difference. Simple knowledge _____ facts has its value. To know who won the battle _____ Poltava, or when the umpteenth opus _____ Mozart was first performed, may win $64,000 or some other sum _____ the possessor _____ this information, but I believe educators _____ general are a little embarrassed _____ the assumption that the acquisition _____ such knowledge constitutes education.

Exercise 3: Punctuation

Rewrite the following passage, putting in appropriate punctuation and capitalizing words at the beginning of sentences.

this reminds me of a forceful statement made by a professor of agronomy in my freshman year in college whatever knowledge I gained in his course has departed completely but I remember how with World War I as his background he was comparing factual information with ammunition he wound up his little discourse with the exhortation don't be a damned ammunition wagon be a rifle I believe most educators would share this sentiment that knowledge exists primarily for use

Verb Tenses

The following are the most frequently used English verb tenses:

I am studying English right now.
(the present continuous tense: used for action going on at the present moment)

---

*May be omitted by basic writing students.

*I **study** English every night.*
(the present habitual tense: used for action done repeatedly, as a habit)

*I **will study** English tomorrow.*
(the future tense: used for action in the future; *going to* is also used for this purpose: *I **am going to study** English tomorrow*.)

*I **studied** English yesterday.*
(the simple past tense: used to describe past action, except when the following tenses are used)

*I **was studying** English at eight o'clock last night.*
(the past continuous tense: used for action going on at a particular time in the past)

*I **have studied** English for two years.*
(the present perfect tense: used for an action begun in the past and continuing up to now, or as an "indefinite" past tense. See page 47 for further explanation)

Exercise 4

Imagine that you are in a particular place (at home, at the beach, in a restaurant, etc.). Write a paragraph describing the place and telling what you and the other people are doing there. You will have to use the present tense of *be* and the *present continuous tense* in most of the sentences.

Exercise 5

Rewrite the paragraph you wrote for exercise 4 in the past. Begin by saying "Yesterday . . .," "Last weekend . . .," etc. You will have to use the past of *be* and the *past continuous tense* in most of the sentences.

Exercise 6

Write a paragraph about what you usually do on a typical day (or just in the morning, in the afternoon, in the evening, or on Saturday, on Sunday, in the summer, when you have free time). You will have to use the present habitual tense in most of the sentences.

Exercise 7

Rewrite the paragraph you wrote for exercise 6 in the past. Begin by saying "Yesterday . . .," "Last weekend . . .," etc. You will have to use the simple past tense in most of the sentences.

Exercise 8

Rewrite the paragraph you wrote for exercise 6 in the future. Begin by saying "Tomorrow . . .," "Next weekend . . .," etc. You will have to use the future tense in most of the sentences.

The Present Perfect Tense

The present perfect tense (I *have studied* English) is confusing to many students. Some students use the present perfect tense when they should use the simple past tense, or they use the present tense when they should use the present perfect. The best general rule is to use the simple past tense when speaking or writing about the past unless there is a special reason why you need to use the present perfect tense. The present perfect tense must be used in two situations:

1. To describe action beginning in the past and continuing up to the present; the time words *for* and *since* are often used in this case:

    question: *José, how long **have** you **been** in New York?**
    answer: *I **have been** here **for** two years.*

    question: *Maria, **since** when **have** you **lived** in Brooklyn?*
    answer: *I **have lived** here **since** 1978.*

    question: *Victor, how long **has** your father **worked** for General Motors?*
    answer: *He **has worked** for them **for** three years.*

2. As an "indefinite past" (an exact time is not mentioned; the action occurred some-time before now); the words *already, yet, ever, never* are often used in this case:

    question: *Joseph, **have** you **ever visited** the Statue of Liberty?*
    answer: *Yes I **have.***

    question: *Theresa, **have** you **ever seen** the movie "Jaws"?*
    answer: *No, I **haven't seen** it **yet,** but I would like to.*

    question: *George, how many times **have** you **been** absent this semester?*
    answer: *I **have been** absent about four times, but I will try not to be any more.*

Exercise 9

Put the verbs in the following sentences in the correct tense, present perfect or simple past.

1. Helen (study) English last night.
2. She (study) English for the last three years.
3. I (not finish) my chemistry homework yet.
4. I (finish) my English homework two hours ago.
5. George (go) to that restaurant many times.
6. He (go) there with me last weekend.
7. I already (buy) all my presents for Christmas.
8. Last year I (not buy) my presents until two days before Christmas.

---

*Notice that we use a form of *have (has/have)* and the *past participle* of a verb *(been, written, gone, done, worked, studied, finished, learned)* to make the present perfect tense.

9. I (not feel) very well this week.

10. I (have) a cold last week.

Exercise 10

Ask a classmate, "What have you done in the past five years that you are happy about?" and "Why are you happy about these things?" Your classmate will have up to five minutes to answer, saying things like "I have moved to a new neighborhood. I am happy about this because . . . ." Then, your classmate will ask you the same questions and you will have up to five minutes to answer. After this, write two paragraphs, one about what you have done and one about what your classmate has done. You will have to use the present perfect tense in some of the sentences.

Other Perfect Tenses

Some other "perfect tenses" (using *have* and the *past participle* of a verb) in English are:

1. the present perfect continuous tense:
    I **have been studying** biology for two years.
    (I am still studying biology now.)

2. the past perfect tense:
    I **had studied** English for two years before I came to the U.S.
    (used for action completed before a definite time in the past)

Reminder: The most common tense used to describe past action is the *simple past tense*. Use the simple past tense unless there is a special reason to use another past tense.

Exercise 11: Proofreading

In the following paragraph, errors are *not* underlined, but are indicated in the margin. Find the errors, then rewrite the paragraph, correcting the errors.

v. form	When I look back on the years I was spent in school, I don't re-
run-on	member feeling that I had a purpose for being there, I was there
t.	because I have to be there. My elementary school teachers seemed
pron.	more like babysitters than teachers to me; in fact, I don't remember his
comb.	teaching me anything. I loved to read as a child. I believe I got some sort
frag.	of education. More than anything else, from reading on my own. In
t.	junior high school and high school, my teachers at least had seemed to
comb.	know something about their subject. It wasn't usually a subject that I
run-on	wanted to know about, I had no clear career goal and very few
pron./v.pl.	teachers communicated to me a good reason for learning what he was
	"teaching," other than "Learn it because I'm telling you to learn it."

WRITING

Maybe, as Rogers suggests, most educators feel that what we learn in school should be useful, or maybe they don't. Even if they do, it's not easy to decide what is useful to learn. Think about *your* purpose in getting an education. Why are you in school? How is school useful or important to you? Make an informal outline of why school is (or is not) important to you, such as the following:

> School has not been useful to me
> — here because I have to be here
> — boring teachers
> — no reason to learn the subjects

Tell one or more of your classmates about your purpose(s) for being in school, then write a paragraph about it. Make the first sentence of the paragraph your topic sentence. (It could be "My main reason for being in school is _____," or "My three main reasons for being in school are _____".) Then go on to discuss or explain the topic sentence. See the paragraph on page 132 as a model.

Proofreading

After writing your paragraph, proofread it, particularly checking for the types of errors that *you* have trouble with.

Part Two
ESSAYS

JOBS

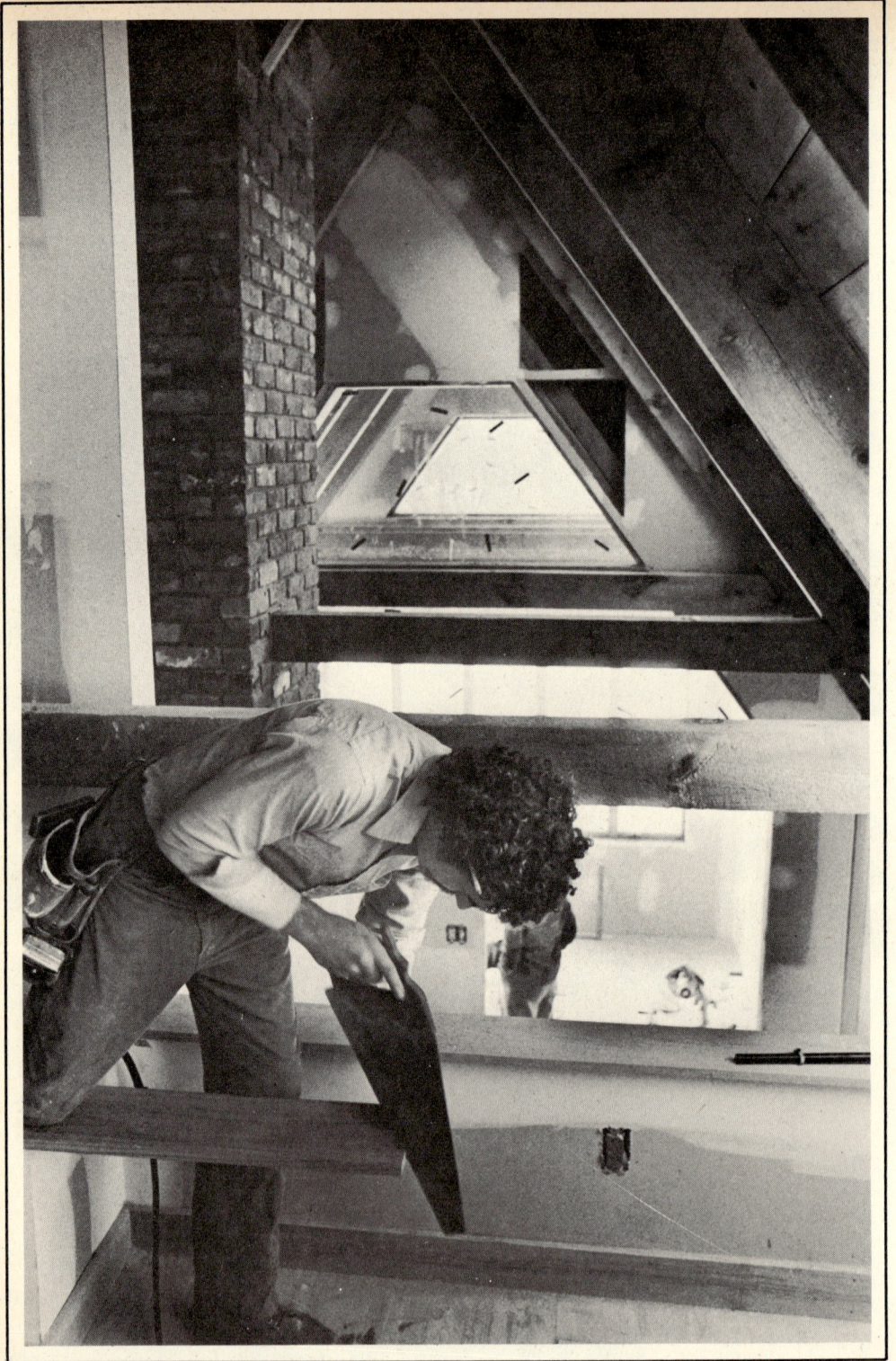

SIX

GETTING A JOB

Much of our time as adults we spend doing a job. It would be nice if this job were a satisfying activity, one that allowed us to use our abilities and to be useful to our fellow man. Unfortunately, as Paul Goodman points out, not everyone can find a job of this sort.

from *Growing Up Absurd*
Paul Goodman

It's hard to grow up when there isn't enough man's work. There is "nearly full employment" (with highly significant exceptions), but there get to be fewer jobs that are necessary or unquestionably useful; that require energy and draw on some of one's best capacities; and that can be done keeping one's honor and dignity. In explaining the widespread troubles of adolescents and young men, this simple objective fact is not much mentioned. Let us here insist on it.

By "man's work" I mean a very simple idea, so simple that it is clearer to ingenuous° boys than to most adults. To produce necessary food and shelter is man's work. During most of economic history most men have done this drudging° work, secure that it was justified and worthy of a man to do it, though often feeling that the social conditions under which they did it were not worthy of a man, thinking, "It's better to die than to live so hard" — but they worked on. When the environment is forbidding, as in the Swiss Alps or the Aran Islands, we regard such work with poetic awe.° In emergencies it is heroic, as when the bakers of Paris maintained the supply of bread

simple

hard and boring

amazement and respect

during the French Revolution, or the milkmen did not miss a day's delivery when the bombs recently tore up London.

necessary for survival

At present there is little such subsistence° work. In *Communitas* my brother and I guess that one-tenth of our economy is devoted to it; it is more likely one-twentieth. Production of food is actively discouraged. Farmers are not wanted and the young men go elsewhere. (The farm population is now less than 15 per cent of the total population.) Building, on the contrary, is immensely needed. New York City needs 65,000 new units a year, and is getting, net,° 16,000. One would think that ambitious boys would flock° to this work. But here we find that building, too, is discouraged. In a great city, for the last twenty years hundreds of thousands have been ill housed, yet we do not see science, industry, and labor enthusiastically enlisted° in finding the quick solution to a definite problem. The promoters are interested in long-term investments, the real estate men in speculation, the city planners in votes and graft.° The building craftsmen cannily° see to it that their own numbers remain few, their methods antiquated,° and their rewards high. None of these people is much interested in providing shelter, and nobody is at all interested in providing new manly jobs.

total/rush in large numbers

joined

bribes/cleverly
old-fashioned

American society has tried so hard and so ably to defend the practice and theory of production for profit and not primarily for use that now it has succeeded in making its jobs profitable and useless.

Comprehension Questions

1. According to Goodman, what is "man's work"?
2. Why is it important to do "man's work"?
3. Why don't many people work on construction?
4. What is the result of the American emphasis on production for profit, not for use?

Form

The preceding passage is a formal essay, including a first paragraph stating the main idea of the entire essay (the *introduction*), middle paragraphs explaining and support-ing the main idea (the *body*), and a final paragraph repeating the main idea (the *conclusion*). Look at the diagram on page 55 to see the three parts of the essay.

Many *introductions* begin with a *general comment,* which informs the reader of the topic of the essay, and end with a *thesis sentence,* giving the main idea of the essay. Introductions do not have to end with a thesis sentence, but this is a good way to lead into the rest of the essay. An introduction can be fairly short (3 or 4 sentences will do).

Each *middle paragraph* usually has a *topic sentence* (giving the main idea of the *paragraph,* not of the essay), which is supported with examples, explanation, statis-tics, or a story. It is important to include specific details; paragraphs with generalities and no specific information are boring. Middle paragraphs should be 4 to 7 sentences long.

AN ESSAY

A. Introduction

> General opening comment
>
> Thesis sentence (main idea
> of the entire essay)

B. Body

> First supporting idea

> Second supporting idea

> Third supporting idea

C. Conclusion

> Thesis repeated
>
> General closing comment

Many *conclusions* begin by repeating the *idea of the thesis sentence* (not using exactly the same words), and end with a *general comment.* They should give the reader the feeling that the essay is finished. Do not end with a new idea that needs explanation, but rather with a comment that seems to "sum up" what you have said in the essay. Like introductions, conclusions can be short (2-3 sentences).

The essay at the beginning of this chapter could be outlined as follows:

intro./thesis: It's hard to grow up when there isn't enough man's work. (in par. 1)
body: What is "man's work"? (par. 2)
                 — producing necessary food and shelter
                 — done throughout history
                 — sometimes heroic (examples: bakers of Paris, milkmen in London)
                 Why isn't man's work available? (par. 3)
                 — 1/10, maybe 1/20 of present work
                 — no work in food production
                 — no work in building
conclusion: Jobs profitable but useless. (par. 4)

Rhetorical Devices

◨ The repetition of *that*-clauses in paragraph 1 stresses the positive aspects of work which are not available in today's jobs.

◨ The repetition of "man's work" at the beginning of paragraph 2 and of "work" at the beginning of paragraph 3 ties both paragraphs to the thesis sentence of the essay ("It's hard to grow up when there isn't enough man's *work*").

◨ The word *as* is used before an example in paragraph 2 ("In emergencies it is heroic, *as* when the bakers of Paris maintained the supply of bread during the French Revolution"). *For example* or *for instance* could also be used in this sentence.

◨ In paragraph 2 *food* and *shelter* are mentioned ("To produce necessary *food* and *shelter* is man's work") and in paragraph 3 Goodman explains first that production of *food* is discouraged and second that production of *shelter* (building) is discouraged.

◨ In paragraph 3 Goodman lists a large number of groups who are not interested in promoting building: science, industry, labor, promoters, real estate men, city planners, building craftsmen. The effect is that there seems to be a social conspiracy against young people who would try to find meaningful work.

GRAMMAR AND SENTENCE STRUCTURE

Exercise 1: Sentence Ordering

Put the following sentences in the correct order.

1. In emergencies it is heroic, as when the bakers of Paris maintained the supply of bread during the French Revolution.
2. During most of economic history most men have done this drudging work, secure that it was justified and worthy of a man to do it.
3. To produce necessary food and shelter is man's work.
4. By "man's work" I mean a very simple idea, so simple that it is clearer to ingenuous boys than to most adults.
5. When the environment is forbidding, as in the Swiss Alps or the Aran Islands, we regard such work with poetic awe.

Exercise 2: Prepositions*

Fill in the correct prepositions (then check the passage at the beginning of this chapter).

It's hard to grow _____ when there isn't enough man's work. There is "nearly full employment" (_____ highly significant exceptions), but there get to be fewer jobs that are necessary or unquestionably useful; that require energy and draw _____ some _____ one's best capacities; and that can be done keeping one's honor and dignity. _____ explaining the widespread troubles _____ adolescents and young men, this simple objective fact is not much mentioned. Let us here insist _____ it.

Exercise 3: Punctuation

Rewrite the following passage, putting in appropriate punctuation and capitalizing words at the beginning of sentences.

at present there is little such subsistence work in Communitas *my brother and I guess that one-tenth of our economy is devoted to it it is more likely one-twentieth production of food is actively discouraged farmers are not wanted and the young men go elsewhere the farm production is now less than 15 per cent of the total population building on the contrary is immensely needed New York City needs 65,000 new units a year and is getting net 16,000 one would think that ambitious boys would flock to this work but here we find that building too is discouraged*

Articles: The Indefinite Article (<u>a</u>/<u>an</u>)

Many students of English as a second language have difficulty in using the English articles *a/an* (the indefinite article) and *the* (the definite article). This is a serious problem since these words are used in practically every English sentence. There are some general rules that will help you to avoid errors. The rules depend on your knowing whether a noun is "countable" or "non-countable."

1. **countable nouns**
   An example of a countable noun is the word *book*: we can count books and the

---

*May be omitted by basic writing students.

word has a plural form made by adding "s" (Jim has two books). Following are a
few countable nouns and their plural forms:

singular form	plural form
chair	chairs
student	students
pen	pens
man	men
woman	women
child	children
person	people

The article *a* (*an* before a vowel sound — a, e, i, o, u, or "silent h") is used with a
singular countable noun to mean "one" of a certain type of thing:

*There is **a** book on the desk.*
*I am sitting in **a** chair.*
*I met **an** interesting man last night.*
*John is **a** good student.*

With plural nouns, the word *some,* or *no article* at all, is used.

*There are **some** books on the desk.*
We are sitting on chairs.
*I met **some** interesting men last night.*
John and Bill are good students.

No article is used with "general meaning" (You can buy pens in a stationary store);
some is used with "specific meaning" (I need to buy *some* pens today).

2. **Non-countable nouns**

   Non-countable nouns in English include *liquids* (water, wine, beer), *powders*
   (sugar, flour, sand), *gases* (air, oxygen), and *abstract ideas* (love, hate, jealousy,
   intelligence). They have no plural form.*

   With non-countable nouns, we never use *a/an. No article* is used with general
   meaning and *some* with specific meaning:

   I like sugar.
   *Please give me **some** sugar.*

   Wine goes well with spaghetti.
   *I need to buy **some** wine.*

   Everyone needs love.

The Definite Article

We use the article *the* when we are talking about something that is definite *in the
mind of our listener* (that is, the listener knows what thing or person we are talking

---

*Many words in English can be used either as countable or as non-countable nouns. For example, we can say
"I like *coffee*" (non-countable) or "Please give me two *coffees*" (countable).

about). For example, I can't say to someone "The book was good" unless the person knows what book I am talking about. I could say, "The book that you gave me last week was good." Following are some situations where *the* is used:

1. **for second mention** (use "a" for first mention):
   *I saw **a** good movie last night. **The** movie was about college life.*
2. **with restrictive phrases or clauses:**
   ***The** notebook **on the desk** is mine.*
   ***The** house **that John lives in** is big.*
3. **for a unique thing** (there is only one thing that the listener can think of):
   ***The** sun is hot today.*
   ***The** teacher is absent today.* (meaning the teacher of *this* class)

Do **not** use *the* with general meaning. The following examples are correct:
   Milk is good for you.
   Students must work hard.

Do **not** use *the* before:

1. certain place expressions:
   *I go to **school.** (class, work, church, town, bed)*
2. names of games:
   *I play **football.** (soccer, baseball, chess)*
3. languages:
   *I speak **Spanish.** (French, Chinese, Russian)*
   But we say, "I speak the *Spanish language."*
4. continents, countries, states, cities, towns:
   *I live in **North America.** (Canada, Ontario, Toronto)*
   EXCEPTIONS: We say the *United States,* the *Soviet Union,* the *Philippines.*
5. streets, avenues, roads, squares, etc.:
   *This store is located on **Forty-Second Street.** (Fifth Avenue, Washington Place, etc.)*
6. parks, lakes, specific mountains:
   *I love **Central Park.** (Lake Michigan, Bear Mountain)*
   But note that we say the *Rocky Mountains,* the *Alps (for a range of mountains) or* the *Mississippi River,* the *Mediterranean Sea,* the *Atlantic Ocean (for bodies of water other than lakes).*
7. possessive pronouns or nouns:
   *I am going to **Charley's** Café. (his house, my apartment)*
8. holidays:
   *We are going to have a party for **Christmas.** (Easter, New Years)*

Exercise 4

Put in articles (*a/an, the*) where necessary. If no article is needed, put an *X* in the blank.

To produce _____ necessary food and shelter is _____ man's work. During most of _____ economic history most men have done this drudging work, secure that it was justified and worthy of _____ man to do it, though often feeling that _____ social conditions under which they did it were not worthy of _____ man, thinking, "It's better to die than to live so hard"—but they worked on. When _____ environment is forbidding, as in _____ Swiss Alps or _____ Aran Islands, we regard such work with _____ poetic awe.

Exercise 5 (to be done in pairs or small groups)

Take out of your pockets, wallet, or purse ten things that you usually carry with you (a comb, a handkerchief, some keys, etc.). Tell your classmates what these things are and why you usually carry them with you. Do *not* use the word *my* but use articles (*a/an, the*) before the names of these things. Then write a paragraph about the ten things and why you carry them, again *not* using the word *my*.

Exercise 6 (to be done in pairs or small groups)

Tell your classmate what you are going to be when you finish school (a teacher, nurse, computer programmer, etc.). Mention three or four things that people in this profession do (Teachers . . .). Will you enjoy this work? Why? After you and your classmate have both done this, write a paragraph about your future profession. (You will write an essay on this topic at the end of the chapter.)

Exercise 7: Proofreading

In the following passage, errors are *not* underlined, but are indicated in the margin. Find the errors; then rewrite the passage, correcting the errors.

art.	I come from family of teachers. My father was a teacher, my sister is
t.	a teacher, and I am a teacher. What are we all finding satisfying about this profession?
t.	Well, for one thing, I considered myself not only a teacher, but also
v.sg./v.sg.	a learner. Being a teacher allow me, in fact force me to be a learner. I
art.	must find the interesting articles or books for my students to read and
run-on/comb.	write about, I must read and react to these books or articles myself. I must have something to share with my students. I must sometimes find
n.pl.	way of helping my students to understand their assignments. I must then
frag./n.pl.	try to understand. And respond to my students' idea.

WRITING

Even though, as Goodman points out, it may be difficult to find meaningful work today, most young people still hope to find such work. What kind of work would *you* find meaningful? (If you have a job, you can speak about the job you have, or about a different job that you would like to have.) Make an informal outline, explaining why you want to have a particular job.

> Advantages of being a teacher
> — continuing to be a learner
> — not a routine job
> — a "people job"

Tell one or more of your classmates about the job you would like to have, then write an *essay* about it. Begin with an *introductory paragraph* having a *thesis sentence* telling what kind of job you would like. Try to write three *middle paragraphs,* each one focusing on one advantage of doing this sort of work. Finally, write a *concluding paragraph* summing up what you have said in your essay. You may use the essay on page 133 as a model.

Proofreading

After writing your essay, use the Rhetorical Checklist on page 138 to make sure that your essay has the correct form. Then check the grammar, particularly looking for the types of errors that *you* have trouble with.

SEVEN

MONEY

Even if you aren't in love with your job, at least it's a way to make money. And everyone knows how important money is. In fact, maybe it is too important! True, you need money to live on, but Robert Gould, in the following essay, explains that this isn't the only reason why people, especially men, consider money important.

from "Measuring Masculinity by the Size of a Paycheck"
Robert E. Gould

In our culture money equals success. Does it also equal masculinity? Yes—to the extent that a man is too often measured by his money, by what he is "worth." Not by his worth as a human being, but by what he is able to earn, how much he can command on the "open market."

In my psychiatric practice I have seen a number of male patients through the years, of all ages, who have equated moneymaking with a sense of masculinity. Peter G., for example. He was 23 years old, very inhibited, and socially inept.° Raised in a strict, religious home, he had very little contact with girls and virtually no dating experience until his second year of college. He was sure that no woman would find him attractive unless he was making good money. In analysis° it became evident that he was painfully insecure and unsure of his abilities in any area. Money was his "cover": if he flashed° a roll of bills, no one would see how little else there was to him. He needed expensive clothes, a big sporty car, and a thick wallet . . . . Money would show women he could give them what they needed, and thereby get him what he thought he needed, "a beautiful girl . . . ." His idea that women were essentially passive and looking to be

incapable, ineffective

psychological therapy, treatment

showed

63

win sexually (slang)

sexual ability

leading oneself to
defeat

very masculine men
(colloq.)

cleverness

new places

defeat

very full, fat

taken care of by a big, strong male demanded that he "make" good
money before he could "make"° the woman of his dreams.

This kind of thinking is often reinforced by both men and women who
have bought the myth that endows a moneymaking man with sexiness
and virility,° and is based on man's dominance, strength, and ability to
provide for and care for "his" woman. We have many cultural models of
this unrealistic and frequently self-defeating° image of masculinity. Hollywood has gone a long way to reflect and glorify it in such figures as the
John Wayne-style cowboy, the private eye, war hero, foreign correspondent, lone adventurer—all "he-men"° (a phrase that in its redundancy
seems to "protest too much") who use physical strength, courage, and
masculine wiles° to conquer their worlds, their villainous rivals, and their
women. Money rarely has anything to do with it.

But in real life . . . few women have much concern about men like that.
After all, there are few frontiers° to conquer, or international spy rings to
crack,° or glorious wars to wage. All that is left, for the real-life, middle-
class man is the battle for the bulging° wallet.

Comprehension Questions

1. Why is money important to men?
2. What is a "myth"?
3. What myth is mentioned in paragraph three?
4. What was John Wayne an example of?
5. In real life, what kind of men are many women interested in?

Form

This essay could be outlined as follows:

thesis: To many people, money equals masculinity (par. 1)
                — the example of Peter G. (par. 2)
                    — little social experience
                    — needed money for self-confidence
                    — hoped money would attract a woman
                — the myth of the dominant man (par. 3)
                    — sexy, virile, able to provide
                    — models: John Wayne-style cowboy, etc.
                    — money not related to these models
conclusion: — men like these models not real (par. 4)
                — only "the battle for the bulging wallet" is left

Rhetorical Devices

☐   In the introduction, Gould uses the interesting technique of asking a question
and answering it (Does money also equal masculinity? Yes—to the extent that

. . .). Another interesting technique is using a question like this as the thesis sentence, then answering it in the middle paragraphs (see the essays on page 133).

◻ The first sentence of paragraph 2 is connected to the thesis (mentioning "*moneymaking*" and "*masculinity*"), as is the first sentence of paragraph 3 (mentioning "*moneymaking*" and listing some supposedly masculine qualities).

◻ Gould effectively uses *details* in discussing what Peter G. thought he needed (a roll of bills, expensive clothes, a big sporty car, a thick wallet) and by giving examples of Hollywood's masculine models (the John Wayne-style cowboy, the private eye, war hero, foreign correspondent, lone adventurer).

◻ The expression *such . . . as* is used in paragraph 3 with a number of examples ("in *such* figures *as* the John Wayne-style cowboy, . . ."). The word *like* could also be used in this case (in figures *like* the John Wayne-style cowboy, etc.).

◻ The explanatory expression *after all* is used in paragraph 4 ("Few women have much concern about men like that. *After all,* there are few frontiers to conquer, . . ."). Other explanatory expressions are *really, to tell the truth, when you think of it, in fact, as a matter of fact.*

GRAMMAR AND SENTENCE STRUCTURE

Exercise 1: Sentence Ordering

Put the following sentences in the correct order.

1. Peter G., for example.
2. In my psychiatric practice I have seen a number of male patients through the years, of all ages, who have equated moneymaking with a sense of masculinity.
3. He was sure that no woman would find him attractive unless he was making good money.
4. Raised in a strict, religious home, he had very little contact with girls and virtually no dating experience until his second year of college.
5. He was 23 years old, very inhibited, and socially inept.

Exercise 2: Prepositions*

Fill in the correct prepositions (then check the passage at the beginning of this chapter).

This kind _____ thinking is often reinforced _____ both men and women who have bought the myth that endows a moneymaking man _____ sexiness and virility, and is based _____ man's dominance, strength, and ability to provide _____ and care _____ "his" woman. We have many cultural models _____ this unrealistic and frequently self-defeating image _____ masculinity.

---

*May be omitted by basic writing students.

Exercise 3: Articles*

Put in articles (*a/an, the*) where necessary. If no article is needed, put an *X* in the blank.

_____ money was his cover: if he flashed _____ roll of bills, no one would see how little else there was to him. He needed _____ expensive clothes, _____ big sporty car, and _____ thick wallet. . . . _____ money would show _____ women he could give them what he thought they needed, and thereby get him what he thought he needed, "_____ beautiful girl." His idea that _____ women were essentially passive and looking to be taken care of by _____ big, strong male demanded that he "make" _____ good money before he could "make" _____ woman of his dreams.

Exercise 4: Punctuation

Rewrite the following passage, putting in appropriate punctuation and capitalizing words at the beginning of sentences.

in my psychiatric practice I have seen a number of male patients through the years of all ages who have equated moneymaking with a sense of masculinity Peter G. for example he was 23 years old very inhibited and socially inept raised in a strict religious home he had very little contact with girls and virtually no dating experience until his second year of college he was sure that no woman would find him attractive unless he was making good money

Word Forms

Many words in English have different "forms"; the one required in a particular sentence depends on the "part of speech" required (verb, noun, adjective, or adverb):

> *John is an **intelligent** student.* (adjective)
> *His **intelligence** helps him to get good grades.* (noun)
> *He speaks **intelligently.*** (adverb)

> *In the past, women **depended** on men to support them.* (verb)
> *Today many women do not want to be **dependent** on men.* (adjective)
> *Women are seeking **independence.*** (noun)

Exercise 5

Fill in the correct forms of the given words in the following sentences. Use each word only one time.

_____

*May be omitted by basic writing students.

masculine	attract	measure	succeed
masculinity	attractive	measurement	success
	attractively		successful

1. In our society money equals _____ .
2. Men feel they need a lot of money in order to _____ .
3. Mr. Jones has just been made president of his company; he is a _____ man.
4. We sometimes _____ a man by his money.
5. This is not a fair _____ of his worth.
6. Many men feel insecure about their _____ .
7. They feel that they can show they are _____ by making a lot of money.
8. Men are interested in _____ women.
9. Women _____ men by wearing nice clothes.
10. This is why many women feel they must dress _____ .

Exercise 6

Give the requested forms of the words below the passage (use a dictionary if necessary). Then, with the form that you have given, make up a sentence that is related to the passage.

*This kind of **thinking** is often **reinforced** by both men and women who have bought the myth that endows a moneymaking man with **sexiness** and **virility**, and is based on man's **dominance, strength,** and **ability** to **provide** for and care for "his" woman.*

example: thinking/verb: _____think_____

sentence: Many men *think* that women will like them only if they make a lot of money.

1. reinforce/ noun: _____
   sentence:

2. sexiness/ adjective: _____
   sentence:

3. virility/ adjective: _____
   sentence:

4. dominance/ verb: _____
   sentence:

5. strength/ adjective: _____
   sentence:

6. ability/ adjective: _____
   sentence:

7. provide/ noun: _____
   sentence:

Sentence Variety

If you wish to write well, your sentences should have variety. Some sentences should be long, and some short. Your sentences should not all follow a "subject-predicate" pattern, but should begin in different ways, including:

1. **with a prepositional phrase:**
   As a child, I knew only the stone city. — Mario Puzo

2. **with an infinitive phrase:**
   In order to experience this identity, it is necessary to penetrate from the periphery to the core. — Erich Fromm

3. **with a participial phrase** (using a present or past participle):
   Having compassion for the helpless one, man begins to develop love for his brother. — Erich Fromm

   Raised in a strict, religious home, Peter G. had very little contact with girls . . . until his second year of college. — Robert E. Gould

4. **with an adverb:**
   Often father would utter idle threats. — Margaret Mead

5. **with an adverb clause:**
   When I got to New Hampshire, . . . I nearly went crazy with the joy of it. — Mario Puzo

6. **with a sentence connector:**
   And there I would stand in the hot sun, wishing I was anyplace else in the world. — Peter Candell

Exercise 7

Rewrite the following sentences, *not* beginning with the subject of the sentence.

1. You should read the newspaper to find out what is happening in the world.
2. I can buy anything I need in my neighborhood.
3. I met Jane while riding home on the subway.
4. Jim left the room quietly.
5. I don't like my job because my boss is such an unpleasant person.
6. My wife says, despite this, that I shouldn't quit my job.
7. You must study hard in order to get good grades.
8. Bill called his girlfriend when he got home.

9. Bob seems to spend a lot of money although he doesn't earn much.

10. The man looked for his car keys anxiously.

11. There is a nice view from this window.

12. This apartment is expensive because of the view.

Exercise 8: Proofreading

In the following passage, errors are *not* underlined, but are indicated in the margin. Find the errors; then rewrite the passage, correcting the errors.

w. form	No one would argue, I think, that money is unimportance. There are
t.	certain things that human beings are needing—food, shelter, perhaps
v.pl.	medical care—and these things costs money. But if one has enough
n.pl.	money to live on, to pay for the basic essential of life, is it important to
run-on	have a lot more money than that, will your life improve in proportion to the
t.	amount of money that you are having?
v.sg./run-on	Well, there are no denying that money can buy a lot maybe you don't
v.pl.	need much money to pay for shelter, but how about if you wants a nice
frag.	apartment in a nice neighborhood. Or if you want to buy a house. The fact
	is that people do get on each other's nerves if they are crowded together.
	Members of a married couple or members of a family are likely to get
w. form	along better if they are not constant tripping over each other, if each can
v. form	finds a little privacy from time to time.

WRITING

In the essay at the beginning of this chapter, Gould suggests that money is more important to some people than it should be. Men, for example, ought to be able to feel worthwhile and attractive to the opposite sex even if they don't make a lot of money. Yet I think no one will argue that money is unimportant. I have heard people say "Money can't buy happiness, but I'd rather be rich and unhappy than poor and unhappy!" How important do *you* think money is? Why is it important, or unimportant? Following are a number of questions related to money.

1. How important is money?

2. How much money do I need to make? Why?

3. What would I do if I had a lot of money?

4. Would I want my husband (or wife) to make a lot of money? Why?

5. Is the salary an important aspect of a job? Why?

6. Discuss the life of someone who makes a lot of money. Is he/she happy? Why? (This can be either someone who you know personally, or a famous person that you know about.)

7. Discuss the life of someone that you know who doesn't make a lot of money. Is he/she happy? Why?

8. Do I admire men who make a lot of money? Why?

9. Do I admire women who make a lot of money? Why?

Choose one of these questions and make an informal outline for an essay such as the following:

> How important is money?
> — important for a nice house or apartment
> — important for entertainment
> — not good to work all the time for money

Tell one or more of your classmates your ideas about the topic that you chose; then write an essay about it, with an introduction, a body, and a conclusion. You may use the essay that begins on page 133 as a model.

Proofreading

After writing your essay, use the Rhetorical Checklist on page 138 to make sure that your essay has the correct form. Then check the grammar, particularly looking for the types of errors that *you* have trouble with.

PROBLEMS
IN SOCIETY

EIGHT

WORLD PROBLEMS

Speaking of "progress" suggests that our world has changed for the better. Surely, things have changed, but when you look at the world today, you may well wonder if all the changes have been for the better.

from "Developing Global Units for Elementary Schools"
Donald Morris

Just for a moment, imagine that you are a first-class passenger on a huge spaceship traveling at a speed of 100,000 kilometers per hour. You discover that the ship's environmental system is faulty.° Some passengers are dying due to poisonous gases in their oxygen supply. Also there is a serious shortage of provisions—food supplies are being used up and the water supply is rapidly becoming polluted due to breakdowns in the waste and propulsion systems.

In the economy sections passengers are crowded together. Conditions are bad, especially for the children. Many are seriously ill. The ship's medical officers are able to help few of the sick and medicines are in short supply.

Mutinies° and fighting have been reported in some sections. Hopefully this conflict can be contained, but there is fear that the violence may spread into the other compartments.

The spacecraft has an overall destruct system, with the controls carefully guarded by a special technical crew. Unfortunately, the number of technologists who know how to set off the destruct system has increased,

° not working correctly

° rebellions

73

and there is great concern over what might happen if the fighting does spread.

We could go on, but the point is: What would you do if you were on that spaceship? Now that you have "imagined," are you ready to face reality? You are on such a spaceship right now—Spaceship Earth!

Comprehension Questions

1. What are some problems on the imaginary spaceship described in this passage?
2. What is Morris really describing?
3. How is our "environmental system" faulty?
4. What does Morris mean by the "economy sections"?
5. What "destruct system" is he talking about?

Form

This essay could be outlined as follows:

```
thesis:     Describing an "imaginary" spaceship
            — conditions in first class (par. 1)
              — faulty environmental system
              — shortage of provisions
            — conditions in economy sections (par. 2)
              — crowded
              — many are ill
            — mutinies and fighting (par. 3)
            — the destruct system (par. 4)
conclusion: — This is Spaceship Earth (par. 5)
```

Rhetorical Devices

☐ An informal tone is achieved by using the second person singular ("Imagine that *you* are a first-class passenger . . .").

☐ The first sentence of each paragraph has a word related to "spaceship": *spaceship* (par. 1), *sections* (par. 2), *sections* (par. 3), *spacecraft* (par. 4), *spaceship* (par. 5). This repetition ties the paragraphs together.

☐ The expression of addition *also* is used in paragraph 1 ("Some passengers are dying due to poisonous gases . . . . *Also,* there is a serious shortage of provisions"). Other expressions of addition are *moreover, furthermore, besides that, in addition to that.*

☐ The adverb *hopefully* is used in paragraph 3 ("*Hopefully,* this conflict can be contained"). The same idea could be expressed in other ways: "The crew hope that this conflict can be contained" or "It is hoped that this conflict can be contained."

GRAMMAR AND SENTENCE STRUCTURE

Exercise 1: Sentence Ordering

Put the following sentences in the correct order.

1. Also, there is a serious shortage of provisions.
2. Some passengers are dying due to poisonous gases in their oxygen supply.
3. Just for a moment, imagine that you are a first-class passenger on a huge space-ship traveling at a speed of 100,000 kilometers per hour.
4. You discover that the ship's environmental system is faulty.

Exercise 2: Prepositions*

Fill in the correct prepositions (then check the passage at the beginning of this chapter).

_____ the economy sections passengers are crowded together. Conditions are bad, especially _____ the children. Many are seriously ill. The ship's medical officers are able to help few _____ the sick and medicines are _____ short supply.

Mutinies and fighting have been reported _____ some sections. Hopefully this conflict can be contained, but there is fear that the violence may spread _____ the other compartments.

Exercise 3: Articles*

Put in articles (*a/an, the*) where necessary. If no article is needed, put an *X* in the blank.

_____ spacecraft has _____ overall destruct system, with _____ controls carefully guarded by _____ special technical crew. Unfortunately, _____ number of _____ technologists who know how to set off _____ destruct system has increased, and there is _____ great concern over what might happen if _____ fighting does spread.

Exercise 4: Punctuation

Rewrite the following passage, putting in appropriate punctuation and capitalizing words at the beginning of sentences.

just for a moment imagine that you are a first-class passenger on a huge spaceship traveling at a speed of 100,000 kilometers per hour you discover that

---

*May be omitted by basic writing students.

the ship's environmental system is faulty some passengers are dying due to poisonous gases in their oxygen supply also there is a serious shortage of provisions food supplies are being used up and the water supply is rapidly becoming polluted due to breakdowns in the waste and propulsion systems

Passive Verb Forms

Sometimes we may feel that the "object" of a verb is more important than its "subject." For example, the following sentence is odd:

> Someone fixed my car last night.

The sentence is odd because I am probably not so much interested in "someone" as in "my car." If I want to give "my car" more emphasis, I can move it to the front of the sentence and use a *passive verb form:*

> My car was fixed last night.

We can include the original subject with the word *by* (My car was fixed *by* someone last night) or just omit it if we feel it is unimportant.
   We make passive verb forms in the following way:

active verb forms	passive verb forms
Someone *is fixing* my car now.	My car *is being fixed* now.
Someone *fixes* my car every month	My car *is fixed* every month.
Someone *will fix* my car tomorrow.	My car *will be fixed* tomorrow.
Someone *fixed* my car yesterday.	My car *was fixed* yesterday.
Someone *was fixing* my car at 10 o'clock this morning.	My car *was being fixed* at 10 o'clock this morning.
Someone *has fixed* my car twice this month.	My car *has been fixed* twice this month.

To make passive verb forms:

1. move the original object of the verb to the beginning of the sentence;
2. use the verb *be* in the same tense as the verb of the original sentence (*is fixing/is being, fixes/is,* etc.);
3. use the past participle of the original verb (something is being *fixed, written, done,* etc.).

Note: It is not considered good style to use passive verb forms too much in English. Use active verb forms unless there is a special reason to use a passive—for example, when the original object is more important than the original subject.

Exercise 5

Change the following sentences from active to passive. Eliminate the original subject if it is unimportant.

1. The teacher divided the class into two groups.
2. The city will construct a new highway next year.
3. The state is improving the transportation system.
4. Someone was repairing this road last week.
5. We teach foreign languages in American schools.
6. Doctors have not found a cure for cancer.
7. The owners sold this house last week.
8. The laundry workers are washing my clothes now.
9. We don't respect old people very much in the United States.

Exercise 6

Change the following sentences from passive to active. You will have to provide a subject where the original subject has been omitted.

1. The class was being observed by the principal when I came in.
2. One thousand students are admitted to this college every year.
3. This car was taken off the market by Ford due to safety hazards.
4. The garbage is not being collected often enough in my neighborhood.
5. The school budget has not yet been approved by the president.
6. An international conference on peace will be held next year at the United Nations.
7. Final exams are taken by students in January and May.
8. My wallet was stolen by a pickpocket last week.
9. A new grocery store has been opened by Mr. Jones.

Exercise 7 (to be done in pairs or small groups)

Tell one or more classmates about what has been done to improve your neighborhood in the last few years. Also tell about what should be done to improve it in the future. Then write a paragraph about this, using passive verb forms in some of the sentences.

Exercise 8 (to be done in pairs)

Who is someone that you depend on (your mother, father, sister, brother, a friend, teacher, boss, etc.)? Using passive verb forms, mention three or four things that are done for you by this person. What do you do for this person? After you and your classmate have both done this, write a paragraph about the person that you depend on.

Exercise 9: Proofreading

In the following passage, there are 11 errors: 3 verb form, 2 word form, 2 articles, 1 tense, 2 subject-verb agreement, and 1 run-on. Find the errors; then rewrite the passage, correcting the errors.

> Certainly, one of problems that everyone living in New York City has to be concern about is crime. Every time you turn on radio or look through the newspaper, you heard about muggings, murders, rapes, burglaries. It make you feel like not turning on the radio. However, instead of trying to pretend that this problem don't exist, you're better off trying to do something about it.
>
> Much can being done at the neighborhood level to control crime on my block—in Park Slope, Brooklyn—we have an actively association that has had some succeed in fighting crime. One thing we have did is to get in touch with the local police precinct.

WRITING

It's not a cheerful prospect to think about all the problems mentioned in the essay at the beginning of this chapter: air pollution, water pollution, food shortages, overpopulation, sickness, fighting between countries, the danger of nuclear war. It makes you want to get off the ship. Since we cannot get off the ship, however, we had better face these problems and try to solve them. Choose *one* of the above-mentioned problems, or another problem of your own choice (it does not have to be a "world problem," but can be a neighborhood problem, a school problem, or a family problem), and think about how to solve it. Make an informal outline such as the following:

    Fighting crime
        — cooperation with the police
        — making your house secure

Tell one or more of your classmates about the problem you chose and the solutions you propose; then write an essay about it, with an introduction, a body, and a conclusion. You may use the essay on page 134 as a model.

Proofreading

After writing your essay, use the Rhetorical Checklist on page 138 to make sure that your essay has the correct form. Then check the grammar, particularly looking for the types of errors that *you* have trouble with.

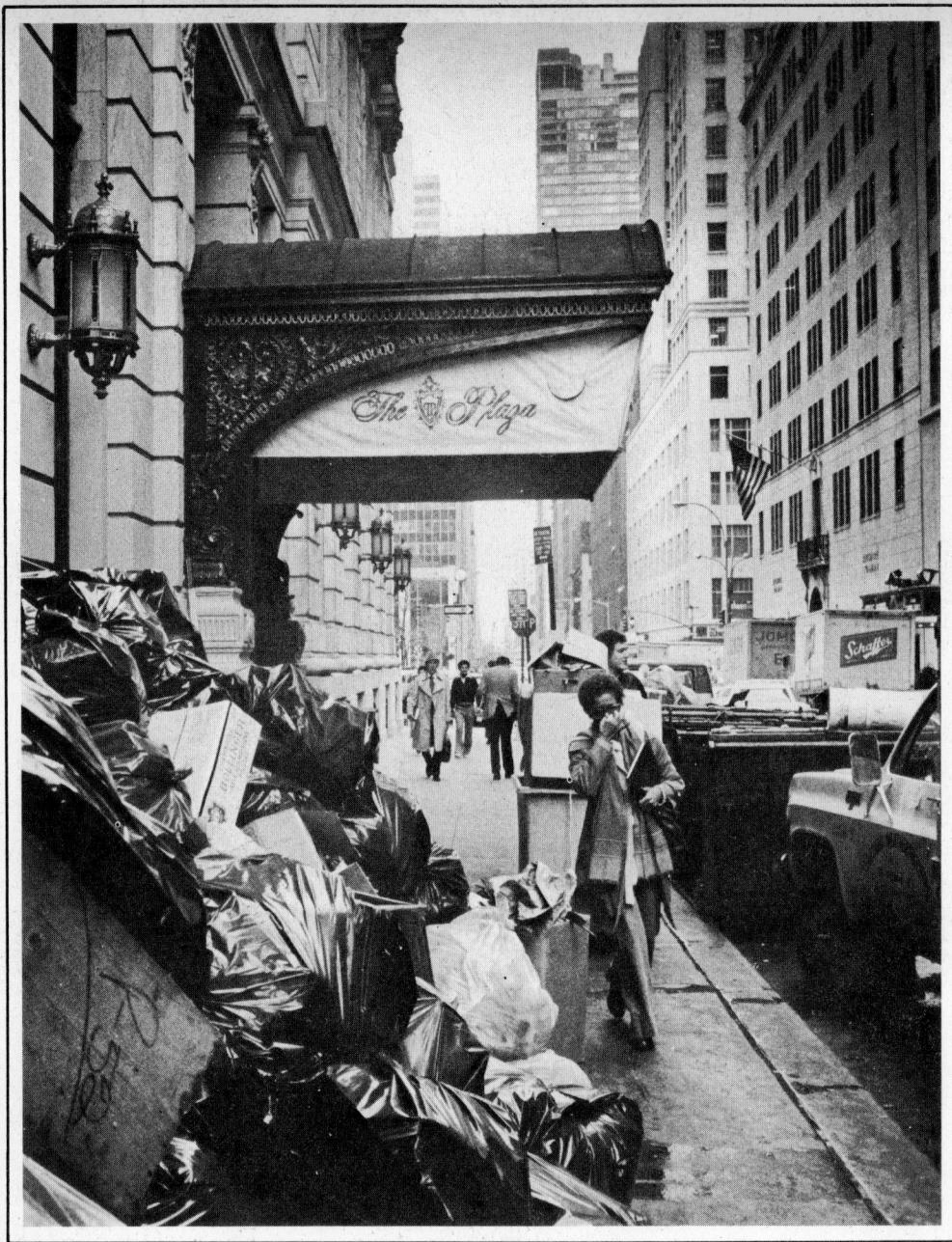

NINE

CITIES

One change that has occurred in recent history is that more and more people are moving to cities. Unfortunately, as Eric Sevareid points out in the following essay, more people may be living in cities today than in medieval times (about 1000 years ago), but the living conditions haven't improved much.

from "Dirt, Grime, and Cruel Crowding"
Eric Sevareid

One way to go quietly insane is to think hard about the concept of eternity.° Another way, for anyone living in a megalopolis° like New York, is to think hard about "progress." The eerie sensation comes over one that true progress reached the end of its cable some years ago and is now recoiling upon us, an unstoppable juggernaut° smashing masses of human beings back toward medieval conditions of life.

The streets are littered with cigarette and cigar butts, paper wrappings, particles of food, and dog droppings. How long before they become indistinguishable from the gutters° of medieval towns when slop pails° were emptied from the second-story windows?

Thousands of New York women no longer attend evening services in their churches. They fear assault° as they walk the few steps from bus or subway station to their apartment houses. The era of the medieval footpad° has returned, and, as in the Dark Ages, the cry for help brings no assistance, for even grown men know they would be cut down before the police could arrive.

A thousand years ago in Europe, acres of houses and shops were de-

time going on forever/very large city

powerful force

sides of the street/pails filled with garbage

attack

robber who travels on foot

81

molished and their inhabitants forced elsewhere so that great cathedrals
could be built. For decades° the building process soaked up all available
skilled labor; for decades the townspeople stepped around pits in the
streets, clambered° over ropes and piles of timber, breathed mortar dust,
and slept and woke to the crashing noise of construction.

The cathedrals, when finished, stood half-empty six days a week, but
most of them had beauty.

Today, the ugly office skyscrapers go up, shops and graceful homes
are obliterated,° their inhabitants forced away, and year after year New
Yorkers step around the pits, stumble° through the wooden catwalks,°
breathe the fine mist of dust, absorb the hammering noise night and day,
and telephone in vain° for carpenter or plumber.

And the skyscrapers stand empty two days and seven nights a week.
This is progress.

At the rush hour,° men outrun old women for the available cab; the
strong bodily crush back the weak for a place to stand in suffocating bus
or subway car, no less destructive of human dignity than a cattle wagon in
the time of Peter the Great. When the buses and subway cars began, they
represented progress. Great parking garages are built, immediately filled
with cars; the traffic remains as before, and that is progress. The re-
nowned° New York constructionist, Robert Moses, builds hundreds of
miles of access highways, and they are at once crammed° bumper to
bumper with automobiles as long as locomotives, carrying an average of
about two human beings apiece.

Parkinson's general law applies here too, for vehicles will always increase in direct proportion to the increase in spaces to hold them. So skyscrapers and boxlike apartment houses will increase as the money to build
them increases.

But it's progress.

The secret, terrible fact is that progress, in all measurable terms of
human effort, grace, and self-respect, ended some years ago in the great
ant-hill cities. The juggernaut° of time and effort has turned around and is
now destroying the recent progressive past.

Side glosses (left margin, top to bottom):
periods of ten years
climbed
destroyed
trip /narrow places to walk through
in . . . with no success
rush . . . crowded time of traveling to or from work
famous
filled
powerful force

Comprehension Questions

1. How does Sevareid feel about "progress"?
2. Why do people in cities not help each other to fight crime?
3. How are today's skyscrapers similar to medieval churches?
4. Do our buses and subways represent progress today? Why?

Form

The preceding essay makes a comparison. In the introduction, Sevareid suggests that
life in New York City today is like life in a medieval town, and he questions whether

"progress" has occurred (that is, whether things have improved since then). The essay could be outlined as follows:

thesis:	True progress has not occurred: conditions of life are like those in medieval times (par. 1)
	— streets are littered, like medieval gutters (par. 2)
	— people fear assault, as they did in medieval times (par. 3)
	— people were inconvenienced due to cathedrals in medieval times (par. 4)
	— people are inconvenienced due to office skyscrapers today (par. 5)
	— buses and subways are crowded, like cattle wagons in the past (par. 6)
	— "Parkinson's law" (that work will expand to take up whatever time you have to do it in) applies for vehicles and skyscrapers (par. 7)
conclusion:	— Progress ended some years ago (par. 8)

Rhetorical Devices

☐ Notice that this essay follows the common pattern of beginning with a short introduction, having the thesis sentence of the essay as the last sentence of the introduction.

☐ Following paragraphs 4, 5, and 7 are separate sentences, which are really part of the preceding paragraphs. By separating these sentences, Sevareid gives them special emphasis. As someone who is just beginning to write essays, however, you should generally not write separate sentences like this but should always write *in paragraphs.*

☐ Notice the "parallel structure" of paragraphs 4 and 5. Paragraph 4, which discusses the construction of cathedrals, includes the series of verbs *stepped, clambered,* and *breathed,* and ends with a separate sentence using the expression *stood half-empty.* Paragraph 5, which discusses the construction of skyscrapers, includes the series of verbs *step, stumble, breathe,* and ends with a separate sentence using the expression *stand empty.*

☐ The essay is connected by repetition of terms related to medieval times: *medieval conditions* (par. 1), *medieval towns* (par. 2), *medieval footpad* (par. 3), *a thousand years ago* (par. 4).

☐ The essay is also connected by repetition of the word *progress:* "true *progress* reached the end of its cable" (par. 1), "this is *progress*" (par. 5), "that is *progress*" (par. 6), "but it's *progress*" (par. 7), "destroying the recent *progressive* past" (par. 8).

☐ The causal word *for* is used in paragraph 3 ("The cry for help brings no assistance, *for* even grown men know they would be cut down") and again in paragraph 7 ("Parkinson's general law applies here too, *for* vehicles will always increase in direct proportion to the increase in spaces to hold them"). Other causal words are *because* and *since.*

☐ The expression of purpose *so that* is used in paragraph 4 ("their inhabitants forced elsewhere *so that* great cathedrals could be built"). Another expression of purpose is *in order that.*

GRAMMAR AND SENTENCE STRUCTURE

Exercise 1: Sentence Ordering

Put the following sentences in the correct order.

1. When the buses and subway cars began, they represented progress.
2. The traffic remains as before, and that is progress.
3. The strong bodily crush back the weak for a place to stand in suffocating bus or subway car, no less destructive of human dignity than a cattle wagon in the time of Peter the Great.
4. At the rush hour, men outrun old women for the available cab.
5. Great parking garages are built, immediately filled with cars.

Exercise 2: Prepositions*

Fill in the correct prepositions (then check the passage at the beginning of this chapter).

The streets are littered _____ cigarette and cigar butts, paper wrappings, particles _____ food, and dog droppings. How long before they become indistinguishable _____ the gutters _____ medieval towns when slop pails were emptied _____ the second-story windows?

Thousands _____ New York women no longer attend evening services _____ their churches. They fear assault as they walk the few steps _____ bus or subway station _____ their apartment houses.

Exercise 3: Articles*

Rewrite the passage, putting in articles (*a/an, the*) where necessary. If no article is needed, put an *X* in the blank.

One way to go quietly insane is to think hard about _____ concept of _____ eternity. Another way, for anyone living in _____ megalopolis like _____ New York, is to think hard about _____ "progress." _____ eerie sensation comes over one that _____ true progress reached _____ end of its cable some years ago and is now recoiling upon us, _____ unstoppable juggernaut smashing masses of _____ human beings back toward _____ medieval conditions of life.

Exercise 4: Punctuation

Rewrite the following passage, putting in appropriate punctuation and capitalizing words at the beginning of sentences.

a thousand years ago in Europe acres of houses and shops were demolished

---

*May be omitted by basic writing students.

and their inhabitants forced elsewhere so that great cathedrals could be built for decades the building process soaked up all available skilled labor for decades the townspeople stepped around pits in the streets clambered over ropes and piles of timber breathed mortar dust and slept and woke to the crashing noise of construction the cathedrals when finished stood half-empty six days a week but most of them had beauty

Comparing with Adjectives and Adverbs

Comparative and *superlative* forms of adjectives and adverbs are made in the following ways.

1. **short adjectives and adverbs:**
   a. add *-er* to make comparative forms:
      This book is longer than that one.
      It is hotter today than it was yesterday.

      George runs faster than John.
      Mr. Brown works harder than Mr. Smith.

   b. add *-est* to make superlative forms:
      This is the longest book I have ever read.
      Today is the hottest day we have had in a long time.

      George runs the fastest of all the students in the class.
      Mr. Brown works the hardest of all the employees.

2. **long adjectives and adverbs:**
   a. use *more . . . than* or *less . . . than* to make comparative forms:
      Bob is more intelligent than his brother.
      Sue is less attractive than Jane.

      Bob speaks more intelligently than his brother.
      Jane works less conscientiously than Sue.

   b. use *the most* or *the least* to make superlative forms:
      Bob is the most intelligent student in his class.
      Sue is the least attractive girl in her class.

      Bob spoke the most intelligently of all the speakers.
      Jane has worked the least conscientiously of all the girls.

3. **as . . . as:**
   To indicate that two things are the same in a certain way, use *as . . . as* with both short and long adjectives:
      This book is as long as that one.
      Chemistry is as difficult as physics.

      My car goes as fast as his.
      I drive as carefully as John.

4. **irregular forms:**

simple form	comparative	superlative
good (or "well")	better (than)	(the) best
bad (or "badly")	worse (than)	(the) worst

far	farther (than)	(the) farthest
many (or "a lot")	more (than)	(the) most
a little	less (than)	(the) least

Exercise 5 (to be done in pairs or small groups)

Tell one or more classmates about how two of your friends or two members of your family (two brothers, sisters, mother and father, etc.) are the same or different. Then write a paragraph comparing these two people.

Exercise 6 (to be done in pairs or small groups)

Tell one or more classmates how *you* are similar to or different from someone that you know (either a friend or a relative). Then write a paragraph comparing yourself to this other person.

Direct Speech and Reported Speech

The following are examples of *direct speech:*

Grandma never said, "Do this because Grandma says so." — Margaret Mead

During most of economic history most men have done this drudging work, . . . thinking, "It's better to die than to live so hard." — Paul Goodman

As Simone Weil expressed it so beautifully: "The same words can be commonplace or extraordinary according to the manner in which they are spoken." — Erich Fromm

Often in writing, we do not quote the exact words that a speaker used, but we use *reported speech* instead. The above quotes would be written as reported speech in the following way:

Margaret Mead's grandmother never said that Margaret should do something because her grandmother said so.

During most of economic history most men have done this drudging work, thinking it was better to die than to live so hard.

Simone Weil said that the same words can be commonplace or extraordinary, according to the manner in which they are spoken.

In changing *direct speech* into *reported speech* there is often:

1. tense change:

direct speech:	*Bill said, "I **am** going to school."*
reported speech:	*Bill said that he **was** going to school.*
direct speech:	*John said, "I **can't** speak to you now because I **have to** leave.*
reported speech:	*John said he **couldn't** speak to me then because he **had to** leave.*

2. word order change:

direct speech: *Bill asked John, "**Have you** eaten lunch yet?"*
reported speech: *Bill asked John if **he had** eaten lunch yet.*

direct speech: *The man asked me, "What time **is it**?"*
reported speech: *The man asked me what time **it was.***

Exercise 7

Change the following sentences from direct to reported speech.

1. John told me, "I understand how you feel."
2. I asked Joan, "Where do you live?"
3. Jane said, "I don't like traveling."
4. Bill asked me, "When will you call me?"
5. I asked Mary, "Are you busy tonight?"
6. Mary said, "I can't see you tonight."
7. Bob said, "I am not satisfied with my job."
8. The man asked me, "Do you have a dime?"
9. The woman asked, "What day is it?"
10. I asked Jane, "What do you want to do?"

Exercise 8

Talk to a classmate for five minutes about the place where you live. (What do you like about it? What do you dislike? etc.) After your conversation is finished:

a. Write it in direct speech as a dialogue.
b. Rewrite the dialogue in reported speech.

Exercise 9: Proofreading

In the following passage there are 14 errors: 1 compar. form, 1 v. form, 2 w. form, 2 art., 3 tense, 3 S-V agreement, and 2 run-ons. Find the errors; then rewrite the passage, correcting the errors.

> And pace of life was so much more slower and more pleasant in Tunisia. I used to sat down in a cafe at the end of the day and just stay there for hours and hours, friends would come and went. We might decide to go eat in a restaurant, or to go to a movie, or just to sit there and chat. In the New York people doesn't usually do that. Everyone are always going somewhere, and is usual late to where they are going. Why, if you tried walking slowly in the streets, you'd be run over by the mad hordes even if you sit in a cafe, chances are that you were looking at your watch and worrying about been late for a movie, or about being late for the babysitter. It seem that rush and worried are just in the air.

WRITING

In the essay at the beginning of this chapter, Eric Sevareid compares life in New York today to life in medieval towns, and concludes that not much progress has been made. Among the *points of comparison* he mentions are *dirty streets, fear of crime,* and *inconvenient construction.* You are going to write your own "comparison essay." Take one of the following topics, or another comparison topic of your own choice:

1. Life in the city and life in the country
2. Two places where I have lived
3. Two places that I have visited
4. Comparing a place now and in the past
   (10 years ago, 50 years ago, 100 years ago, etc.)
5. Comparing life now and in the past
6. Comparing life in two different places

Think about the topic you chose and make an informal outline such as the following (listing the *points of comparison* you are going to discuss):

> Comparing Menzel Bourguiba (a small town in Tunisia, North Africa) and New York City
> — appreciation of nature
> — pace of life

Tell one or more of your classmates about your topic; then write an essay, with an introduction, a body, and a conclusion. You may use the essay on page 135 as a model.

Proofreading

After writing your essay, use the Rhetorical Checklist on page 138 to make sure that your essay has the correct form. Then check the grammar, particularly looking for the types of errors that *you* have trouble with.

RELATIONSHIPS

TEN

THE FAMILY

Despite the problems in the world today, we still try to lead a good life. What else can we do? Certainly, one of the roads to a good life is a good marriage. Yet that seems to be a hard thing to find these days. Marriage has been under severe stress in recent years, as is shown by the large number of divorces, and Alvin Toffler, in the following essay, tells us that we are in for more changes in the future.

from *Future Shock*
Alvin Toffler

The typical pre-industrial family not only had a good many children, but numerous other dependents as well—grandparents, uncles, aunts, and cousins. Such "extended" families were well suited for survival in slow-paced agricultural societies. But such families are hard to transplant.° They are immobile.

move

Industrialism demanded masses of workers ready and able to move off the land in pursuit of jobs, and to move again whenever necessary. Thus the extended family gradually shed° its excess weight and the so-called "nuclear" family emerged—a stripped-down, portable family unit consisting only of parents and a small set of children. This new style family, far more mobile than the traditional extended family, became the standard model in all the industrial countries.

took off

Super-industrialism, however, the next stage of eco-technological development, requires even higher mobility. Thus we may expect many among the people of the future to carry the streamlining° process a step further by remaining childless, cutting the family down to its most elemen-tal° components, a man and a woman. Two people, perhaps with matched careers, will prove more efficient at navigating through education and so-cial shoals,° through job changes and geographic relocations, than the ordinary child-cluttered family. Indeed, anthropologist Margaret Mead has pointed out that we may already be moving toward a system under which, as she puts it, "parenthood would be limited to a smaller number of families whose principal function would be childrearing," leaving the rest of the population "free to function—for the first time in history—as individuals."

making simple or smooth — streamlining
simple — elemental
rocks, barriers — shoals

A compromise may be the postponement of children, rather than childlessness. Men and women today are often torn in conflict between a commitment to career and a commitment to children. In the future, many couples will sidestep this problem by deferring° the entire task of raising children until after retirement.

putting off — deferring

This may strike people of the present as odd. Yet once childbearing is broken away from its biological base, nothing more than tradition suggests having children at an early age. Why not wait, and buy your em-bryos late, after your work career is over? Thus childlessness is likely to spread among young and middle-aged couples; sexagenarians° who raise infants may be far more common. The post-retirement family could be-come a recognized social institution.

people in their sixties — sexagenarians

Comprehension Questions

1. Why did the "nuclear" family develop?
2. According to Toffler, why would families in the future remain childless?
3. How are people "torn in conflict between a commitment to career and a commit-ment to children"?

Form

The preceding essay is a "classification" of different types of families—past, present, and future. It could be outlined as follows:

thesis: Families change as society changes.
   — extended families were good in agricultural societies (par. 1)
   — the nuclear family developed in industrial societies (par. 2)
   — a childless couple will be better in a super-industrial society (par. 3)
   — couples may postpone having children (par. 4)
   — the post-retirement family could become common (par. 5)

Rhetorical Devices

- Notice the parallelism between the first sentence of paragraph 2, which begins with the word "industrialism" (contrasting with the "agricultural societies" mentioned in the preceding paragraph) and the first sentence of paragraph 3, which begins with the word "super-industrialism."
- The word *thus* expresses result. It is used in paragraph 2 ("Industrialism demanded masses of workers ready to move. *Thus* the extended family shed its excess weight"), in paragraph 3 ("Super-industrialism requires higher mobility. *Thus* we may expect people to carry the streamlining further"), and in paragraph 5 ("Nothing more than tradition suggests having children at an early age. . . . *Thus* childlessness is likely to spread"). Other expressions of result are *therefore, consequently, as a result of that, due to that, because of that.*
- The expression of emphasis *indeed* is used in paragraph 3 ("Two people will prove more efficient than the child-cluttered family. *Indeed,* anthropologist Margaret Mead has pointed out that we may already be moving toward . . . 'a smaller number of families whose functions would be childrearing'"). Other expressions of emphasis are *in fact,* and *as a matter of fact.*
- The word *yet,* which indicates a contrast, is used in paragraph 5 ("This may strike people of the present as odd. *Yet* once childbearing is broken away from its biological base, nothing more than tradition suggests having children at an early age"). Other contrastive expressions are *however* and *nevertheless.*

GRAMMAR AND SENTENCE STRUCTURE

Exercise 1: Sentence Ordering

Put the following sentences in the correct order.

1. Indeed, anthropologist Margaret Mead has pointed out that we may already be moving toward a system under which parenthood would be limited to a smaller number of families whose principal function would be childrearing.

2. Thus we may expect many among the people of the future to carry the streamlining process a step further by cutting the family down to its most elemental components, a man and a woman.

3. Super-industrialism, the next stage of eco-technological development, requires even higher mobility.

4. Two people, perhaps with matched careers, will prove more efficient at navigating through job changes and geographic relocations than the ordinary child-cluttered family.

Exercise 2: Prepositions*

Fill in the correct prepositions (then check the passage at the beginning of this chapter).

   A compromise may be the postponement _____ children, rather than childlessness. Men and women today are often torn _____ conflict between a commitment _____ career and a commitment _____ children. _____ the future, many couples will sidestep this problem _____ deferring the entire task _____ raising children until _____ retirement.

Exercise 3: Articles*

Put in articles (*a/an, the*) where necessary. If no article is needed, put an *X* in the blank.

   _____ industrialism demanded _____ masses of _____ workers ready and able to move off _____ land in _____ pursuit of _____ jobs, and to move again whenever necessary. Thus _____ extended family gradually shed its excess weight and _____ so-called "nuclear" family emerged— _____ stripped-down portable family unit consisting only of _____ parents and _____ small set of _____ children. This new style family, far more mobile than _____ traditional extended family, became _____ standard model in all _____ industrial countries.

Exercise 4: Punctuation

Rewrite the following passage, putting in appropriate punctuation and capitalizing words at the beginning of sentences.

   super-industrialism however the next stage of eco-technological development requires even higher mobility thus we may expect many among the people of the future to carry the streamlining process a step further by remaining childless cutting the family down to its most elemental components a man and a woman two people perhaps with matched careers will prove more efficient at navigating through education and social shoals through job changes and geographic relocations than the ordinary child-cluttered family

Modal Verbs

Modal verbs are used before other verbs to express such meanings as "future action" and "possible action." The following modal verbs have the indicated meanings:

   will (future action)   *Vehicles **will** always increase in direct proportion to the increase in spaces to hold them.* — Eric Sevareid

---

*May be omitted by basic writing students.

can (ability)	*She **can** cool their passions or warm their soup with equal competence.* — E. B. White
may (possibility)	*To know who won the battle of Poltava **may** win $64,000 for the possessor of this information.* — Carl R. Rogers
might (weak possibility)	*There is great concern over what **might** happen if the fighting does spread.* — Donald Morris
must (necessity)	*Without being judgmental, we **must** allow these patients to express their anger and dismay.** — Elisabeth Kübler-Ross
should (advisability)	*To such patients, we **should** never say, "Come on now, cheer up."* — Elisabeth Kübler-Ross

The following modal verbs are used in speaking about the past:

would   *Peter G. was sure that no woman **would** find him attractive unless he was making good money.* — Robert E. Gould

could   *He thought money would show women he **could** give them what they needed.* — Robert E. Gould

might   *She feared that he **might** fall down the steep little staircase.* — Margaret Mead

had to   *In the summer of 1956, after he **had to** move from the little house in which all the mementos of his life were in place, he was obviously failing.* — Margaret Mead

Modal verbs are sometimes used with *have* and the *past participle* of a verb:

*The couple **should have waited** for a longer time before having children.* (They are sorry that they didn't wait.)

*Mr. Jones **could have gotten** a promotion, but he didn't want to move to another city.* (He had the opportunity, but he didn't do it.)

*Moving to the city **may have made** life more difficult for Mr. and Mrs. Smith.* (Maybe it made life more difficult.)

*John **must have been** happy when he got his promotion.* (It is almost certain that he was happy.)

---

*Have to has the same meaning as *must.* We could also say, "We *have to* allow patients to express their anger." But *must not* is not the same as *don't have to*: You *must not* steal money (it is necessary not to do it); I *don't have to* work tonight (I can choose to work or not to work).

Exercise 5 (to be done in pairs)

Imagine that a classmate is going to visit your native country (or the city where you were born, or a special place that you have visited). Tell him/her what he/she must do, should do, can do, may want to do, etc. Then write your advice in a paragraph.

Exercise 6

Tell one or more classmates about a mistake that you made in the past. Tell what you did and what you should have done. Then write a paragraph about it.

Exercise 7

a. Imagine that you are a married person who is having some sort of trouble with your marriage. Write a letter to an "advice columnist" explaining what the problem is and asking what you should do about it.
b. Exchange letters with a classmate.
c. Now, imagine that you are the advice columnist. Write a letter responding to your classmate's letter, telling him/her what to do about the problem.
d. Students can read to the class a few of these letters and responses, or summarize them, or the teacher can make them into a printed advice column and hand it out to the class.

Exercise 8: Proofreading

In the following passage there are 11 errors: 2 w. form, 2 art., 3 tense, 2 S-V agr., 1 n.pl., and 1 frag. Find the errors, then rewrite the passage, correcting the errors.

> In Future Shock, Alvin Toffler suggest that, in the future, more and more married couples may chose not to have the children. Or may put off having children for a long time. Because of this, it will be more convenience for these couples to move around to a different jobs in different locations. They will not be, as he puts it, a "child-cluttered family." But is convenience all that a couple should be aim for? And are children mainly a "clutter" to our lives? If our society are in fact heading toward childless for the majority of married couple, I think perhaps we should paused and think about where we are going and if we truly wanting to go there.

WRITING

Introductions and Conclusions

Before writing an essay on the family, let us take a moment to discuss introductions and conclusions. You know that the *introduction* must interest your readers and tell them what the essay is going to be about (state its *thesis*). There are various ways in which you can do this, including:

1. giving some interesting background information
2. making an interesting general comment
3. showing the importance of the topic
4. using a quotation
5. using a question
6. mentioning the ideas that will be discussed in the body of the essay
7. using description or narration (a story)

Notice the techniques used in some of the introductions to the model essays in this book:

Showing the importance of the topic:

It's hard to grow up when there isn't enough man's work. There is "nearly full employment" (with highly significant exceptions), but there get to be fewer jobs that are necessary or unquestionably useful; that require energy and draw on some of one's best capacities; and that can be done keeping one's honor and dignity. In explaining the widespread troubles of adolescents and young men, this simple objective fact is not much mentioned. Let us here insist on it. — Paul Goodman

Using a question:

In our culture money equals success. Does it also equal masculinity? Yes—to the extent that a man is too often measured by his money, by what he is "worth." Not by his worth as a human being, but by what he is able to earn, how much he can command on the "open market." — Robert E. Gould

Using description:

Just for a moment, imagine that you are a first-class passenger on a huge spaceship traveling at a speed of 100,000 kilometers per hour. You discover that the ship's environmental system is faulty. Some passengers are dying due to poisonous gases in their oxygen supply. Also, there is a serious short-age of provisions — food supplies are being used up and the water supply is rapidly becoming polluted due to breakdowns in the waste and propulsion systems. — Donald Morris

Making an interesting general comment:

One way to go quietly insane is to think hard about the concept of eternity. Another way, for anyone living in a megalopolis like New York, is to think hard about "progress." The eerie sensation comes over one that true progress reached the end of its cable some years ago and is now recoiling upon us, an unstoppable juggernaut smashing masses of human beings back toward medieval conditions of life. — Eric Sevareid

Giving some interesting background information:

The typical pre-industrial family not only had a good many children, but numerous other dependents as well—grandparents, uncles, aunts, and cousins. Such "extended" families were well suited for survival in slow-paced

agricultural societies. But such families are hard to transplant. They are immobile. — Alvin Toffler

The *conclusion* of an essay usually *repeats the thesis* and makes a general closing comment or summary statement. The same techniques that are used in introductions can also be used in conclusions. Notice the techniques used in some of the conclusions of the model essays in this book:

Interesting summary statement:
> *American society has tried so hard and so ably to defend the practice and theory of production for profit and not primarily for use that now it has succeeded in making its jobs profitable and useless.* — Paul Goodman

Using a question:
> *We could go on, but the point is: What would you do if you were on that spaceship? Now that you have "imagined," are you ready to face reality? You are on such a spaceship right now—Spaceship Earth!* — Donald Morris

Using a quotation:
> *Only in the love of those who do not serve a purpose, love begins to unfold. Significantly, in the Old Testament, the central object of man's love is the poor, the stranger, the widow and the orphan, and eventually the national enemy, the Egyptian and the Edomite. By having compassion for the helpless one, man begins to develop love for his brother; and in his love for himself he also loves the one who is in need of help, the frail, insecure human being. Compassion implies the element of knowledge and of identification. "You know the heart of the stranger," says the Old Testament, "for you were strangers in the land of Egypt; . . . therefore love the stranger!"* — Erich Fromm

An Essay on the Family

Although we hear these days that the family is "threatened" by the rising rate of divorce, it nevertheless seems likely that the family is here to stay. An institution that has been around as long as the family has will not disappear so quickly. However, it may, as Toffler suggests, undergo some changes. Following are some questions on what the family has been or what it will be, and on your own experience with the family:

1. What do you think families of the future will be like?
2. How are families today different than in the past?
3. What is necessary for a couple to have a good marriage?
4. Why are so many people getting divorced today?
5. Did your parents have a good marriage? Why?
6. Do you know a happily married couple? What makes their marriage good?
7. Do you know a couple that you do not consider happily married? What is wrong with their marriage?

8. If you come from another country, compare marriages in the United States and marriages in your native country.

9. Is it possible for a woman to work and to have a good marriage? Discuss.

10. Discuss the advantages of the "extended" family.

11. Discuss the advantages of the "nuclear" family.

12. Discuss the advantages and/or disadvantages of having children.

13. How can a society make things easier for a couple who both work and have children?

14. Do you think the idea mentioned by Mead of having "a smaller number of families whose principal function would be childrearing" is a good one? Why?

15. Do you think the "post-retirement family," mentioned by Alvin Toffler as a possible future social development, would be a good idea? Why?

Choose one of the questions and make an informal outline such as the following:

> Childlessness is not a good idea
> — you can share pleasures with your children
> — having children makes you more a part of society

Tell one or more of your classmates about your ideas on the topic that you chose; then write an essay about it, with an introduction, a body, and a conclusion. Try to use one of the introduction types mentioned in this chapter. You may use the essay on page 135 as a model.

Proofreading

After writing your essay, use the Rhetorical Checklist on page 138 to make sure that your essay has the correct form. Then check the grammar, particularly looking for the types of errors that *you* have trouble with.

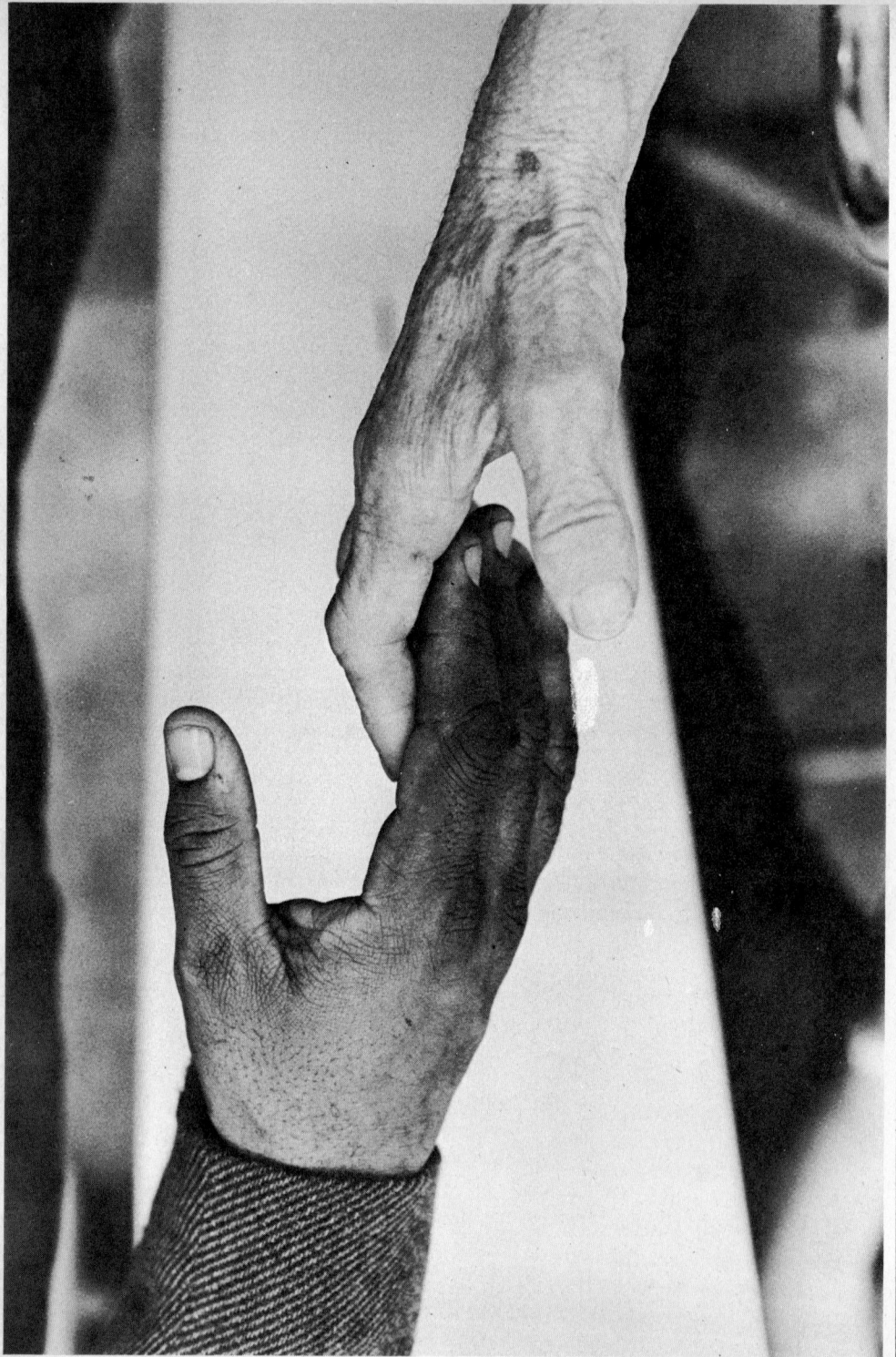

ELEVEN

BROTHERLY LOVE

A good marriage relationship, though hard enough to achieve, should not be all that one seeks. If a married couple are in love only with each other, this "egotism à deux" (Erich Fromm's term) cuts them off from the rest of the world, and is likely to end in unhappiness and divorce. A greater goal is the "brotherly love" described by Fromm in the following essay.

from *The Art of Loving*
Erich Fromm

The most fundamental kind of love, which underlies all types of love, is brotherly love. By this I mean the sense of responsibility, care, respect, knowledge of any other human being, the wish to further his life. This is the kind of love the Bible speaks of when it says: love thy neighbor as thyself. Brotherly love is love for all human beings; it is characterized by its very lack of exclusiveness. If I have developed the capacity for love, then I cannot help loving my brothers. In brotherly love there is the experience of union with all men, of human solidarity, of human at-onement.° Brotherly love is based on the experience that we all are one. The differences in talents, intelligence, knowledge are negligible° in comparison with the identity of the human core common to all men. In order to experience this identity it is necessary to penetrate from the periphery° to the core. If I perceive in another person mainly the surface, I perceive mainly the differences, that which separates us. If I penetrate to the core, I perceive our identity, the fact of our brotherhood. This relatedness from center to center—instead of that from

being as one, together, united

unimportant

outside

101

periphery to periphery—is "central relatedness." Or as Simone Weil expressed it so beautifully: "The same words (e.g., a man says to his wife, 'I love you') can be commonplace or extraordinary according to the manner in which they are spoken. And this manner depends on the depth of the region in a man's being° from which they proceed without the will being able to do anything. And by a marvelous agreement they reach the same region in him who hears them. Thus the hearer can discern,° if he has any power of discernment, what is the value of the words."

inner nature, essence

understand

Brotherly love is love between equals: but, indeed, even as equals we are not always "equal"; inasmuch as we are human, we are all in need of help. Today I, tomorrow you. But this need of help does not mean that the one is helpless, the other powerful. Helplessness is a transitory° condition; the ability to stand and walk on one's own feet is the permanent and common one.

temporary, passing

Yet, love of the helpless one, love of the poor and the stranger, are the beginning of brotherly love. To love one's flesh and blood is no achievement. The animal loves its young and cares for them. The helpless one loves his master, since his life depends on him; the child loves his parents, since he needs them. Only in the love of those who do not serve a purpose, love begins to unfold.° Significantly, in the Old Testament, the central object of man's love is the poor, the stranger, the widow and the orphan, and eventually the national enemy, the Egyptian and the Edomite. By having compassion for the helpless one, man begins to develop love for his brother; and in his love for himself he also loves the one who is in need of help, the frail,° insecure human being. Compassion implies the element of knowledge and of identification. "You know the heart of the stranger," says the Old Testament, "for you were strangers in the land of Egypt; ... *therefore love the stranger!*"

open up

weak

Comprehension Questions

1. What must a person do in order to experience brotherly love?
2. What does Weil mean when she says, "The same words can be commonplace or extraordinary"?
3. Why does the Old Testament emphasize loving the poor, the stranger, the widow and the orphan, and the enemy?

Form

Most of this essay is devoted to a definition of "brotherly love." It could be outlined as follows:

thesis: The most fundamental kind of love is brotherly love.
          — multiple definitions of brotherly love (par. 1)

— how to experience brotherly love (par. 1)
— brotherly love is love between equals (par. 2)
— it is love of the helpless, of those who do not serve a purpose (par. 3)

Rhetorical Devices

☐ Fromm begins a definition with the words *by this I mean* ("The most fundamental kind of love is brotherly love. *By this I mean* the sense of responsibility, care, respect, knowledge of any other human being, the wish to further his life"). Other words and expressions used to define are *means* ("Brotherly love *means* . . ."), *equals, is, implies, is equivalent to, is the same as, refers to, is characterized by, is considered to be, may be defined as.*

☐ Once in paragraph 1 and twice in paragraph 3 Fromm refers to the authority of the Bible to explain what brotherly love is, ending the essay with a quotation from the Old Testament.

☐ In paragraph 3 Fromm uses parallel structure in listing "easy" kinds of love ("the animal loves its young, . . . the helpless one loves his master, . . . the child loves his parents"), and also in listing Old Testament objects of love ("the poor, the stranger, the widow and the orphan, and eventually the national enemy, the Egyptian and the Edomite").

☐ The expression *in order to* is used in paragraph 1 to indicate purpose or intention ("*In order to* experience this identity it is necessary to penetrate from the periphery to the core"). The simple infinitive with "to" could also be used to convey the same meaning (*To* experience this identity it is necessary to penetrate from the periphery to the core).

☐ The expression *inasmuch as* is used in paragraph 2 to indicate a cause and effect relationship ("*inasmuch as* we are human, we are all in need of help"). The words *because* and *since* could also be used here.

GRAMMAR AND SENTENCE STRUCTURE

Exercise 1: Sentence Ordering

Put the following sentences in the correct order.

1. By this I mean the sense of responsibility, care, respect, knowledge of any other human being, the wish to further his life.
2. Brotherly love is love for all human beings.
3. The most fundamental kind of love, which underlies all types of love, is brotherly love.
4. If I have developed the capacity for love, then I cannot help loving my brother.
5. This is the kind of love the Bible speaks of when it says: love thy neighbor as thyself.
6. It is characterized by its very lack of exclusiveness.

Exercise 2: Prepositions*

Fill in the correct preposition (then check the passage at the beginning of this chapter).

_____ brotherly love there is the experience _____ union _____ all men, _____ human solidarity, _____ human _____-onement. Brotherly love is based _____ the experience that we all are one. The differences _____ talents, intelligence, knowledge are negligible _____ comparison _____ the identity _____ the human core common _____ all men. _____ order to experience this identity it is necessary to penetrate _____ the periphery _____ the core.

Exercise 3: Articles*

Put in articles (*a/an, the*) where necessary. If no article is needed, put an *X* in the blank.

_____ same words (e.g., _____ man says to his wife, "I love you") can be commonplace or extraordinary according to _____ manner in which they are spoken. And this manner depends on _____ depth of _____ region in _____ man's being from which they proceed without _____ will being able to do anything. And by _____ marvelous agreement they reach _____ same region in him who hears them. Thus _____ hearer can discern, if he has any power of discernment, what is _____ value of _____ words.

Exercise 4: Punctuation

Rewrite the following passage, putting in appropriate punctuation and capitalizing words at the beginning of sentences.

love of the helpless one love of the poor and the stranger are the beginning of brotherly love to love one's flesh and blood is no achievement the animal loves its young and cares for them the helpless one loves his master since his life depends on him the child loves his parents since he needs them only in the love of those who do not serve a purpose love begins to unfold significantly in the Old Testament the central object of man's love is the poor the stranger the widow and the orphan and eventually the national enemy the Egyptian and the Edomite

Conditional Sentences

Conditional sentences in English usually include an *if*-clause (a clause that begins with *if*) and a second, main clause. Four common types of conditional sentences in English are:

---

*May be omitted by basic writing students.

1. **present habitual:**

    If I perceive in another person mainly the surface, I perceive mainly the differences.

    If I penetrate to the core, I perceive our identity.

    (The present habitual tense is used in both clauses.)

2. **future conditional:**

    If the patient expresses his grief, he will feel more comfortable. — Elisabeth Kübler-Ross

    "If you give me one more year to live, I will be a good Christian."

    (The present tense is used in the *if*-clause, the future tense in the main clause.)

3. **present "unreal" conditional** (imagining something in the present or future):

    If you asked them, most educators would probably say that knowledge exists primarily for use.

    Many ambitious boys would want to be construction workers if jobs were available in this area.

    (The past tense is used in the *if*-clause, the conditional tense in the main clause.)

4. **past "unreal" conditional** (imagining something in the past):

    Puzo would have been happy if he had been able to continue going to the country.

    Peter G. would have felt that he was unattractive to women if he had not made a lot of money.

    (The past perfect tense is used in the *if*-clause, the past conditional tense in the main clause.)

Summary: The four main types of conditional sentences are:

present habitual:	*I study if I have time.*
future:	*I will study tonight if I have time.*
present unreal:	*I would study if I had time.*
past unreal:	*I would have studied last night if I had had time.*

Exercise 5

Complete the following sentences.

1. I take a taxi if . . .
2. I go to sleep early if . . .
3. I will watch TV tonight if . . .
4. I will go to the movies this weekend if . . .
5. I would study harder if . . .
6. I would take a vacation if . . .

7. I would have gone to sleep early last night if . . .

8. I would have written a letter to my parents yesterday if . . .

Exercise 6

What would you like to be (a rich person, a movie star, a famous artist, etc.)? Tell one or more classmates what you would do if you were this type of person; then write a paragraph about it.

Exercise 7

If you could have one wish, what would you wish for? Tell one or more classmates what your wish would be and why; then write a paragraph about it.

Exercise 8: Proofreading

In the following passage there are 11 errors: 2 tense, 2 v. form, 2 w. form, 2 art., 1 S-V agr., 1 run-on, and 1 frag. Find the errors; then rewrite the passage, correcting the errors.

> The religions of the world has produce great books, with great lessons to teach. If we follow what is wrote in the books, the world would certainly be a better place, unfortunately, most people, even so-called "religious" people, do not truly follow the paths of goodness and righteous so beautiful described by their religion.
>
> To many people in United States, the house of worship (church, synagogue, etc.) is more place to socialize than anything else. They come to see and to talk to their friends. To show their fine clothes. They come because "people will talk" if they didn't come.

WRITING

"All you need is love" says a song of the Beatles. Unfortunately, love is not so easy to find. Some people spend their whole lives seeking love and never finding it—not just the very special kind of "brotherly love" that Fromm discusses in his essay at the beginning of this chapter, but any kind of love. Certainly, love is worth thinking about; perhaps thinking about it can help us to understand it, and to find it. Consider the following questions about love.

1. Do you agree with Fromm that "the most fundamental kind of love is brotherly love"? Discuss.
2. Do you have the capacity for brotherly love? Discuss.
3. Describe someone that you know who has the capacity for brotherly love.
4. Describe someone that you know who does not have the capacity for brotherly love.

5. Discuss what the Old Testament (or some other religious book—the New Testament, the Koran, etc.) teaches about love.

6. Does religion as it is practiced today teach people about love? Discuss.

7. What is friendship?

8. Describe a good relationship that you have with a friend.

9. Do you believe that we should love our enemies? Discuss.

10. Describe a romantic love relationship that you have now or had in the past.

11. Some people say that romantic love doesn't last. Do you agree? Discuss.

12. Do you believe that everyone should love the poor? Discuss.

13. How do most people today feel about the poor? Why?

14. A popular song says "Love makes the world go around." Do you agree? Discuss.

15. Do you believe in "love at first sight"? Discuss.

Choose one of these questions to write about, and make an informal outline such as the following:

> People do not follow the principles of their religion
> — like a social club
> — confirm feelings of pride

Tell one or more classmates your ideas on the topic that you chose; then write an essay about it, with an introduction, a body, and a conclusion. You may use the essay on page 136 as a model.

Proofreading

After writing your essay, use the Rhetorical Checklist on page 138 to make sure that your essay has the correct form. Then check the grammar, particularly looking for the types of errors that *you* have trouble with.

GROWING OLD

TWELVE

FACING DEATH

Death is a frightening thing to most people today. Yet it used to be more accepted as a normal part of life. Elisabeth Kübler-Ross has had the courage to study this "taboo"° subject, and to explain how some people have been able to face death without fear.

forbidden, not allowed

from "Facing Up to Death"
Elisabeth Kübler-Ross

Most patients respond to the awareness that they have a terminal° illness with the statement, "Oh no, this can't happen to me." After the first shock, numbness,° and need to deny the reality of the situation, the patient begins to send out cues° that he is ready to "talk about it." If *we*, at that point, need to deny the reality of the situation, the patient will often feel deserted, isolated, and lonely and unable to communicate with another human being what he needs so desperately to share. . . .

leading to death

lack of feeling

signs

Most patients who have passed the stage of denial will become angry as they ask the question, "Why me?" Many look at others in their environment and express envy, jealousy, anger, and rage° toward those who are young, healthy, and full of life. These are the patients who make life difficult for nurses, physicians, social workers, clergymen,° and members of their families. Without justification they criticize everyone.

extreme anger

ministers, priests, rabbis, etc.

What we have to learn is that the stage of anger in terminal illness is a blessing, not a curse. These patients are not angry at their families or at the members of the helping professions. Rather, they are angry at what these people represent: health, pep, energy.

confusion

expressed, let out

Without being judgmental, we must allow these patients to express their anger and dismay.° We must try to understand that the patients have to ask, "Why me?" and that there is no need on our part to answer this question concretely. Once a patient has ventilated° his rage and his envy, then he can arrive at the bargaining stage. During this time, he's usually able to say, "Yes, it is happening to me—*but*." The *but* usually includes a prayer to God: "If you give me one more year to live, I will be a good Christian (or I'll go to the synagogue every day)."

admission

limitation

sad

Most patients promise something in exchange for prolongation of life. Many a patient wants to live just long enough for the children to get out of school. The moment they have completed high school, he may ask to live until the son gets married. And the moment the wedding is over, he hopes to live until the grandchild arrives. These kinds of bargains are compromises, the patient's beginning acknowledgment° that his time is limited, and an expression of finiteness,° all necessary in reaching a stage of acceptance. When a patient drops the *but,* then he is able to say, "Yes, me." At this point, he usually becomes very depressed.° And here again we have to allow him to express his grief and his mourning . . . .

communicate

hold it in

To such patients, we should never say, "Come on now, cheer up." We should allow them to grieve, to cry. And we should even convey° to them that "it takes a brave person to cry," meaning that it takes courage to face death. If the patient expresses his grief, he will feel more comfortable, and he will usually go through the stage of depression much more rapidly than he will if he has to suppress° it or hide his tears.

Only through this kind of behavior on our part are our patients able to reach the stage of acceptance. Here, they begin to separate themselves from the interpersonal relationships in their environment. Here, they begin to ask for fewer and fewer visitors. Finally, they will require only one beloved person who can sit quietly and comfortably near.

pain

sad

This is the time when a touch becomes more important than words, the time when a patient may simply say one day, "My time is very close now, and it's all right." It is not necessarily a happy stage, but the patient now shows no more fear, bitterness, anguish,° or concern over unfinished business. People who have been able to sit through this stage with patients and who have experienced the beautiful feeling of inner and outer peace that they show will soon appreciate that working with terminally ill patients is not a morbid,° depressing job but can be an inspiring experience.

Comprehension Questions

1. According to Kübler-Ross, what are the five stages that one can pass through in facing death?
2. How should we react when terminally ill people get angry? Why?
3. Why shouldn't we say, "Come on now, cheer up."?
4. Is working with terminally ill patients morbid and depressing? Why?

Form

Like the essay at the beginning of Chapter 10, this essay is a sort of classification, this time of the stages one may pass through in facing a terminal illness. It could be outlined as follows:

thesis: There are several stages one may pass through in facing a terminal illness.
- the stage of denial (par. 1)
- the stage of anger (par. 2)
- the importance of accepting this anger (par. 3)
- the stage of bargaining (par. 4)
- the stage of depression (par. 5)
- the importance of accepting this depression (par. 6)
- the stage of acceptance (par. 7)

conclusion: - Working with patients at this stage can be inspiring. (par. 8)

Rhetorical Devices

- Kübler-Ross gives us the feeling that the terminally ill patient is a real person by using quotes: "Oh no, this can't happen to me." (par. 1) "Why me?" (par. 2) "If you give me one more year to live, I will be a good Christian." (par. 3) "Yes, me." (par. 5) "My time is very close now, and it's all right." (par. 8)

- The essay is tied together by the repetition of "Most patients" at the beginning of paragraphs 1, 2, and 5.

- Paragraph 5 is made interesting through presenting examples of "bargains" that patients try to make (until the children get out of school, until the son gets married, until the grandchild arrives).

- When a sentence begins with *only,* as does the first sentence of paragraph 7, the subject-verb order is sometimes reversed ("*Only* through this kind of behavior on our part *are our patients* able to reach the stage of acceptance"). Another example of this type of sentence would be "*Only* by using English a lot *will you* be able to master it."

- In paragraph 7, the word *finally* is used before the last stage to be discussed ("*Finally,* they will require only one beloved person who can sit quietly and comfortably near"). The expressions *at the end* or *at last* could also be used here.

GRAMMAR AND SENTENCE STRUCTURE

Exercise 1: Sentence Ordering

Put the following sentences in the correct order.

1. These are the patients who make life difficult for nurses, physicians, social workers, clergymen, and members of their families.

2. Most patients who have passed the stage of denial will become angry as they ask the question, "Why me?"

3. Without justification they criticize everyone.

4. Many look at others in their environment and express envy, jealousy, anger, and rage toward those who are young, healthy, and full of life.

Exercise 2: Prepositions*

Fill in the correct preposition (then check the passage at the beginning of this chapter).

Most patients respond _____ the awareness that they have a terminal illness _____ the statement, "Oh, no, this can't happen _____ me." _____ the first shock, numbness, and need to deny the reality _____ the situation, the patient begins to send _____ cues that he is ready to "talk _____ it." If *we*, _____ that point, need to deny the reality _____ the situation, the patient will often feel deserted, isolated, and lonely and unable to communicate _____ another human being what he needs so desperately to share.

Exercise 3: Articles*

Put in articles (*a/an, the*) where necessary. If no article is needed, put an *X* in the blank.

_____ most patients promise something in exchange for _____ prolongation of _____ life. Many _____ patient wants to live just long enough for _____ children to get out of _____ school. _____ moment they have completed _____ high school, he may ask to live until _____ son gets married. And _____ moment _____ wedding is over, he hopes to live until _____ grandchild arrives. These kinds of _____ bargains are _____ compromises, _____ patient's beginning acknowledgment that his time is limited, and _____ expression of _____ finiteness, all necessary in reaching _____ stage of acceptance.

Exercise 4: Punctuation

Rewrite the following passage, putting in appropriate punctuation and capitalizing words at the beginning of sentences.

when a patient drops the "but" then he is able to say yes me at this point he usually becomes very depressed and here again we have to allow him to express his grief and his mourning to such patients we should never say come on now cheer up and we should even convey to them that it takes a brave person to cry meaning that it takes courage to face death if the patient expresses his grief he will feel more comfortable and he will usually go through the stage of depression much more rapidly than he will if he has to suppress it or hide his tears

---

*May be omitted by basic writing students.

Verbals

Infinitives ("to go," "to work," etc.) and *gerunds* ("going," "working," etc.), when used as nouns, are called *verbals*.

Infinitives
Infinitives and infinitive phrases (phrases beginning with an infinitive) can be used in the following ways:

1. **subject of a sentence:**
    To know who won the battle of Poltava *may win $64,000 for the possessor of this information.*
2. **object of a verb:**
    Whereas other kids seemed **to look forward to Gym,** *I dreaded it.*
3. **adjective:**
    There are few frontiers **to conquer,** *or international spy rings* **to crack,** *or glorious wars* **to wage.**
4. **adverb:**
    There came a time when I was too old **to be sent away to the country.**

Gerunds
A *gerund* is the *ing*-form of a verb used as a noun. Gerunds and *gerund phrases* can be used in the following ways:

1. **subject of a sentence:**
    Building *is immensely needed.*
2. **object of a verb:**
    Puzo loved **going to the countryside.**
3. **object of a preposition:**
    We do not see science, industry, and labor enthusiastically enlisted in **finding the quick solution to a definite problem.**

Conventional Uses of Infinitives and Gerunds
Some *verbs* that are often followed by *infinitives* are:

advise	expect	persuade
agree	forbid	plan
allow	force	remind
arrange	hope	teach
ask	intend	tell
cause	invite	urge
decide	like	want
deserve	order	
encourage	permit	

Some *verbs* that are often followed by *gerunds* are:

appreciate	finish	prevent
avoid	keep	quit
consider	mind	risk
delay	miss	stop
deny	postpone	suggest
enjoy	practice	

Here are some *expressions with prepositions* that are often followed by *gerunds*. (Infinitives are never used after prepositions.)

accuse someone of	forgive someone for
be accustomed to	insist on
be afraid of	be interested in
apologize for	keep someone from
approve of	object to
believe in	prevent someone from
be capable of	be responsible for
concentrate on	stop someone from
depend on	succeed in
be excited about	be tired of
feel like	be used to
be fond of	

Exercise 5

Complete the following sentences with either infinitive or gerund phrases.

1. I enjoy . . .
2. My parents didn't allow me . . .
3. Next year I plan . . .
4. I am interested in . . .
5. I should stop . . .
6. My friends encourage me . . .
7. I hope to succeed in . . .
8. I'd like to invite you . . .
9. I want you . . .
10. I apologized to my friend for . . .

Noun Phrases

Like infinitive and gerund phrases, *noun phrases* can be used as:

1. **subject of a sentence:**
    Simple knowledge of facts has its value.

2. **object of a verb:**
   I had **no conception of what the countryside could be.**

3. **object of a preposition:**
   I believe educators are a little embarrassed by **the assumption that the acquisition of such knowledge constitutes education.**

Exercise 6

Combine the following sentences by using noun phrases. (Check a dictionary to find the noun forms of the underlined words.)

example:　Third world countries are *developing* industry. This will help their economy.
　　　　　　The *development* of industry will help the economy of third world countries.

1. Church and state are *separated* in the United States. This is a feature of the United States government.
2. John is *able* to speak Spanish. This helps him in his job.
3. George *enjoys* sports. This gives him great pleasure.
4. Bill's wife *complains* constantly. This bothers him a lot.
5. John was *lonely*. This was a serious problem.
6. Jane *conceived* of a new plan. This allowed us to complete our project successfully.
7. Bob *decided* that he could not come. This disappointed us.
8. Margaret Mead's grandmother *influenced* her. This affected Margaret's life a great deal.
9. It is *possible* that it may rain. This could change our plans.
10. My father will *arrive* tonight. We are looking forward to this.

Exercise 7: Proofreading

In the following passage there are 13 errors: 4 v. form, 1 w. form, 1 art., 3 n.pl., 2 S-V agr., and 2 frag. Find the errors, then rewrite the passage, correcting the errors.

> In some country, old people are revere, greatly respected, valued. This make sense when you think about it. Having live so many years, old people have accumulate a good bit of wisdom about life. Not to mention a lot of good story that they can share. Unfortunately, this is not situation that exist in the United States.
>
> Old people often don't have much of a life in the United States. This is particular true in the cities. Many old people, not having much money, can't afford to live in big apartment or in good neighborhoods. So they stay lock up in small rooms. Watching television, cleaning up, and thinking about the good old days.

WRITING

Death is one thing that happens to old people. It isn't however the only thing that old people have to look forward to. Following are some questions about the lives of old people.

1. Did anyone who was close to you ever die of a terminal illness (a grandfather, grandmother, father, mother, friend, etc.)? If so, tell about it.
2. Would you want to work with terminally ill people? Why?
3. If you come from another country, describe the lives of old people in your native country.
4. Describe the lives of old people in the United States.
5. Compare the lives of old people in the United States and in another country.
6. Compare the lives of old people in two different kinds of places (for example, in a city and in the country).
7. Is it good for old people to live in nursing homes? Why?
8. Should old people live with their families? Why?
9. When you grow old, you no longer have the health, pep, and energy of young people. Is it still possible to enjoy your old age? Discuss.
10. How do you feel about the idea of growing old? Do you look forward to it? Why?

Choose one of the above questions and make an informal essay outline such as the following:

> The lives of old people in the U.S.
> — afraid of crime
> — isolated from families
> — some live in special communities

Tell one or more of your classmates your ideas on this topic; then write an essay about it, with an introduction, a body, and a conclusion. You may use the essay on page 137 as a model.

Proofreading

After writing your essay, use the Rhetorical Checklist on page 138 to make sure that your essay has the correct form. Then check the grammar, particularly looking for the types of errors that *you* have trouble with.

THIRTEEN

MEMORIES LIVE ON

Is death really the end? Some religions tell us this is not so—that there is a life after death in which we will be rewarded or punished as we deserve. Yet even if there is no life after death, there will still be memories. In the following passage, Margaret Mead, now herself a memory, discusses her memories of her father's last years.

from *Blackberry Winter*
Margaret Mead

The way in which one's parents grow old matters a great deal. My mother had a severe stroke° and had to learn to talk and walk and relate to the world again. It took her a year to do it, and once she had fully recovered so that she could find any book in the house and locate any name we wanted to know, she died. Her death left my father free because he would not have wanted her to make the long, weary recovery again.

Although he was now alone, he stayed on in the little house into which they had moved on his retirement and in which the rooms were too small for committee meetings. He was as forgetful and as careless of material things as he had always been, but as he did not smoke and the furnace° had an automatic fire arrangement, the principal hazards were to himself and not to the neighbors, in whose children he was deeply interested and for whose sake he had taken down the fence so that they would have more room to play. My youngest sister thought he ought to live in a home for the elderly. She feared that he might fall down the steep° little staircase or be

	illness of the brain
	heater (for the whole house)
	at a high angle

121

run over when he absent-mindedly crossed a street against the light. But I stood out against this. I believed he had a right to run risks in his own way.

odd, unusual
wanting to save money

As my father grew old he became eccentric.° He became parsimonious,° where once he had been open-handed, and complained about the bills run up by the students who sometimes lived with him. He often woke up at four in the morning and started to go out of the house. And he

lost

mislaid° things, but he had never in his life had to find anything or file anything. He told the same stories, but he had always repeated stories, absorbed in the telling and unaware of the listener's expression of recognition or boredom. Now he had fewer stories to tell and told them oftener.

sharp, exact
small class
revolutionary

But the structure of his personality remained intact and his mind was as keen° and fresh, as alert to anything new and interesting as it had ever been. The spring before he died I gave a seminar° to a group who thought of themselves as avant-garde,° but his were the most searching questions.

souvenirs/growing weak

In the summer of 1956, after he had to move from the little house in which all the mementos° of his life were in place, he was obviously failing.° Although his grandchildren found a hotel in which he could live independently and still cause little trouble by leaving his door open or the bath running, because there was someone to watch out for such things, he felt close to the end. When summer school was over, his club, which he had founded and in which he ate lunch every day, closed. He was more alone, but the nephew of an old friend had breakfast with him to be sure that he had one good meal a day, and he himself made a last effort to see those of his old friends who were still alive. He died in his sleep the night he knew I was crossing the Atlantic on my way home.

It was my father, even more than my mother, whose career was limited by the number of her children and her health, who defined for me my place in the world. Although I have acted on a wider stage than either my mother or my father, it is still the same stage—the same world, only with

wider *... greater size*

wider dimensions.° I have been fortunate in being able to look up to my parents' minds well past my own middle years. And I watched my father

grow out of

grow—shed° his earlier racial prejudices and come to respect new institutions of the federal government, such as Social Security and public own-

idea, principle

ership, which he had earlier disapproved of on the premise° that the best government is the least government. Watching a parent grow is one of the most reassuring experiences anyone can have, a privilege that comes only to those whose parents live beyond their children's early adulthood.

Comprehension Questions

1. How did Mead's father feel about the neighbors when he got old?
2. How did he change when he grew older?
3. How did he remain the same?
4. In what ways did he grow in his final years?

Form

This is basically a descriptive and narrative essay in which Mead discusses her father's final years. It could be outlined as follows:

thesis: how her father lived during his final years
          – her mother's last years (par. 1)
          – living in his little house (par. 2)
          – how he changed (par. 3)
          – how he remained the same (par. 4)
          – living in a hotel (par. 5)
conclusion: – how Mead felt about her father's growing old (par. 6)

Rhetorical Devices

☐   Mead interests the reader by describing *in detail* her father's habitual activities (he complained about the bills, woke up at four in the morning and started to go out of the house, made an effort to see his old friends who were still alive).

☐   She tells a few interesting anecdotes (he took down the fence for the neighbor's children; he asked the most searching questions at a seminar that Mead gave; etc.).

☐   The causal word *as* is used in paragraph 2 ("*as* he did not smoke, the principal hazards were to himself and not to the neighbors"). The words *because* or *since* could also be used here.

☐   The word *where* is used in paragraph 3 to indicate contrast ("He became parsimonious, *where* once he had been open-handed"). The words *whereas* or *while* could also be used here.

☐   The illustrative expression *such as* is used in paragraph 6 ("I watched my father grow . . . come to respect new institutions of the federal government, *such as* Social Security and public ownership"). The word *like* could also be used here.

GRAMMAR AND SENTENCE STRUCTURE

Exercise 1: Sentence Ordering

Put the following sentences in the correct order.

1. Her death left my father free because he would not have wanted her to make the long, weary recovery again.

2. My mother had a severe stroke and had to learn to talk and walk and relate to the world again.

3. It took her a year to do it, and once she had fully recovered so that she could find any book in the house and locate any name we wanted to know, she died.

4. The way in which one's parents grow old matters a great deal.

Exercise 2: Prepositions*

Fill in the correct preposition (then check the passage at the beginning of this chapter).

Although he was now alone, he stayed on _____ the little house _____ which they had moved _____ his retirement and _____ which the rooms were too small _____ committee meetings. He was as forgetful and as careless _____ material things as he had always been, but as he did not smoke and the furnace had an automatic fire arrangement, the principal hazards were _____ himself and not _____ the neighbors, _____ whose children he was deeply interested and _____ whose sake he had taken _____ the fence so that they would have more room to play.

Exercise 3: Articles*

Put in articles (*a/an, the*) where necessary. If no article is needed, put an *X* in the blank.

Although his grandchildren found _____ hotel in which he could live independently and still cause little trouble by leaving his door open or _____ bath running, because there was someone to watch out for such things, he felt close to _____ end. When summer school was over, his club, which he had founded and in which he ate lunch every day, closed. He was more alone, but _____ nephew of _____ old friend had breakfast with him to be sure that he had one good meal _____ day, and he himself made _____ last effort to see those of his old friends who were still alive.

Exercise 4: Punctuation

Rewrite the following passage, putting in appropriate punctuation and capitalizing words at the beginning of sentences.

it was my father even more than my mother whose career was limited by the number of her children and her health who defined for me my place in the world although I have acted on a wider stage than either my mother or my father it is still the same stage the same world only with wider dimensions I have been fortunate in being able to look up to my parents' minds well past my own middle years and I watched my father grow shed his earlier racial prejudices and come to respect new institutions of the federal government such as Social Security and public ownership which he had earlier disapproved of on the premise that the best government is the least government

Parallel Structure

A rule of good writing is that sentence elements connected by *and, but,* or *or* should all have *parallel structure* (the same grammatical structure). Avoid errors such as the following:

---

*May be omitted by basic writing students.

INCORRECT: The teacher told the students <u>to buy</u> the book and <u>that they should read</u> the first chapter.

CORRECT: The teacher told the students <u>to buy</u> the book and <u>to read</u> the first chapter.

INCORRECT: Mary likes <u>reading</u> books, <u>listening to</u> music, and <u>she plays</u> tennis.

CORRECT: Mary likes <u>reading</u> books, <u>listening to</u> music, and <u>playing</u> tennis.

INCORRECT: John said <u>that he would come to the party</u> and <u>he would bring some wine</u>.

CORRECT: John said <u>that he would come to the party</u> and <u>that he would bring some wine</u>.

OR: John said he would <u>come to the party</u> and <u>bring some wine</u>.

Exercise 5

Rewrite the following sentences, correcting the errors in parallel structure.

1. Reading the newspaper and to listen to the news on television will let you know what is happening in the world.
2. Students must come to class, take notes, and studying for exams is important too.
3. I have to stay home to write letters and because I want to make a few telephone calls.
4. The teacher said that we should come to his office and he would talk to us.
5. This is more difficult for me than you.
6. John hopes to be a successful businessman and make a lot of money.
7. Bill thinks that he will study accounting and he will get a job as an accountant.
8. Mary enjoys swimming, biking, and she likes to play volleyball.
9. The book is either on the desk or that shelf.
10. I don't know what to do or where I should go.

Wordiness

One final rule of good writing is to not use unnecessary words.

1. Don't repeat words unnecessarily.

   NOT: Professor Brown's lectures were <u>interesting</u> and the books for the course were <u>interesting</u> too.

   BUT: Professor Brown's lectures were interesting and so were the books for the course.

2. Don't use two words having the same meaning.

   NOT: Mr. Smith is a <u>dull</u> and <u>boring</u> man.

   BUT: Mr. Smith is a dull man.

3. Use phrases rather than adverb or adjective clauses where possible.

NOT: <u>Since he was eager to get home</u>, John left the party early.
BUT: Eager to get home, John left the party early.

NOT: The man <u>who is in the corner</u> is the president.
BUT: The man in the corner is the president.

4. Avoid unnecessary *of*-phrases.

NOT: The bookstore <u>of the college</u> is in this building.
BUT: The college bookstore is in this building.

5. Use active rather than passive verb forms.

NOT: The forms <u>were filled out</u> by the students.
BUT: The students filled out the forms.

6. Don't use too many sentences beginning with "it is" or "there is".

NOT: <u>There is</u> a store on the corner that sells newspapers.
BUT: A store on the corner sells newspapers.

7. Don't repeat the same idea in successive sentences.

NOT: Having an education helps you to get a job. You can get a good job if you go to school. An educated person also has a better chance of being employed.
BUT: Having an education helps you to get a good job. For example, a friend of mine . . .

Exercise 6

Remove any unnecessary words from the following sentences.

1. John is an industrious and hard-working student.
2. There was a student in the corner who was reading a newspaper.
3. As I was feeling sick, I decided to leave work early.
4. The tests were taken by the students last week.
5. The books which are required for this course are in the bookstore.
6. John is nice and his sister is nice too.
7. The description of the course is in the catalog of the college.
8. It is very impossible for me to help you now.
9. Jim is rude and ill-mannered.
10. The list of books for this course is in the bookstore of the school.

Exercise 7: Proofreading

In the following passage there are 10 errors: 1 art., 1 tense, 5 S-V agr., 2 frag., and 1 run-on. Find the errors; then rewrite the passage, correcting the errors.

> I just had my thirty-sixth birthday. When I was in my twenties, I think people was getting old. Or at least middle-aged when they was in their thirties, fortunately, now that I am in my thirties, this still seem quite young to me; now I would say that you don't start getting old: Till you're in your forties. But whether I am in fact getting old or not don't bother me very much. I think this is because I am happy with way my life is going and I feel that I am achieving goals that is important to me.

WRITING

I have chosen to end this book not with an essay on death, but with an essay on the fond memories that live on after death. In the sense that we continue to live in the minds of others, death is not really the end. Following are some questions on "recollecting life."

1. What do you want to accomplish in your lifetime? Why?
2. Do you think you will have a successful life? Why?
3. Tell about the life of an old person that you know (a grandfather, grandmother, father, mother, etc.). Do you think this person has had a good life? Why?
4. Discuss the life of a specific famous person (Margaret Mead, John Lennon, John Kennedy, Pablo Picasso, etc.). Did this person have a good life? Why?
5. Compare the lives of two old people that you know. Was one of them more successful? Why?
6. Compare the lives of two famous people. Was one of them more successful? Why?
7. What would you like people to remember or to say about you after you die? Why?
8. Imagine that you are old and are giving advice to a grandson or granddaughter on how to live a good life.

Choose one of these topics and make an informal essay outline such as the following:

> What I want to accomplish in life
> — family life
> — work
> — making the world a better place

Tell one or more of your classmates your ideas on the topic you have chosen; then write an essay about it, with an introduction, a body, and a conclusion. You may use the essay on page 137 as a model.

Proofreading

After writing your essay, use the Rhetorical Checklist on page 138 to make sure that your essay has the correct form. Then check the grammar, particularly looking for the types of errors that *you* have trouble with.

APPENDIXES

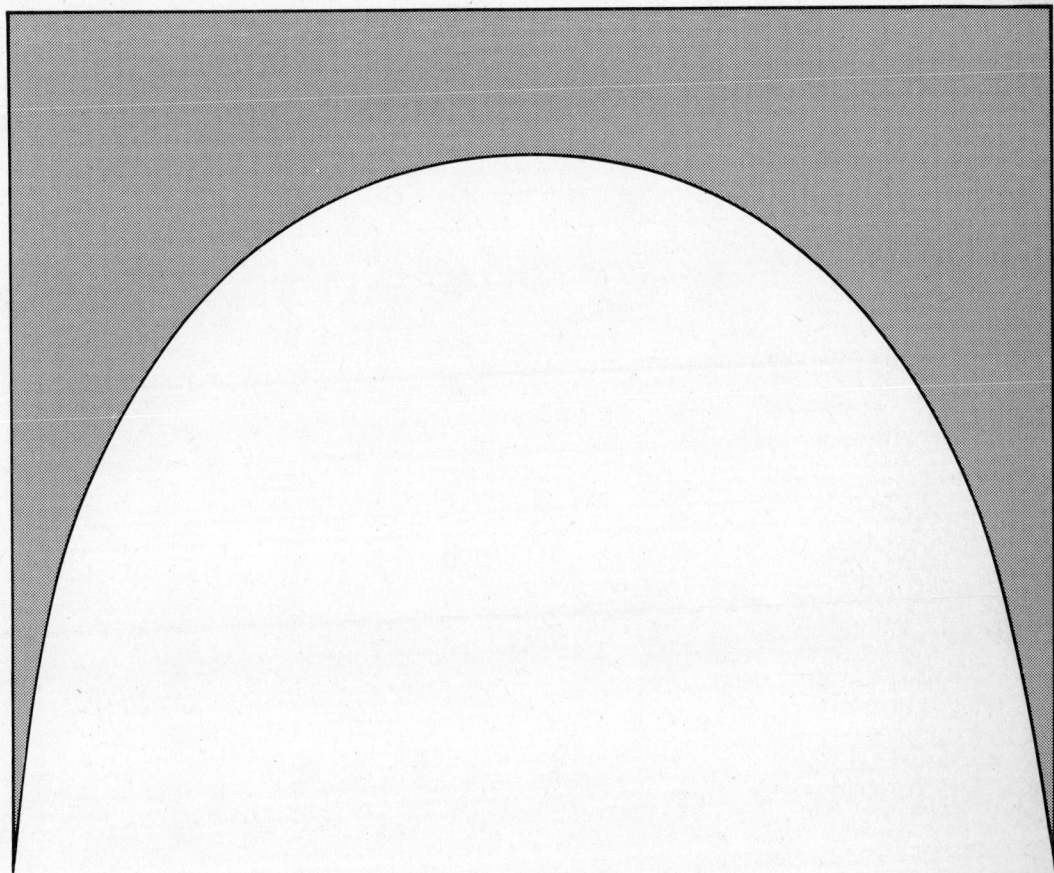

ADDITIONAL MODEL PASSAGES

for Chapter 1   Coney Island

Coney Island, a beach and amusement park area in Brooklyn, was a special place to me when I was a child. My family didn't go that often, but when I knew we were going there, I would feel happy for weeks before the big event. It was a long subway trip to get there from the Bronx, but I hardly noticed it since I was so filled with excitement. The rides were great fun. Coney Island had one of the biggest roller coasters in the world—the Cyclone—and I didn't mind waiting in line a long time for my turn to go on this great attraction. When you got to the top of the giant ferris wheel, you could see all the rides, and the beach and ocean right next to the amusement park. Walking around, you were surrounded by alluring colors and smells: pink cotton candy, giant cherry lollypops with clown faces painted on, huge red jelly-apples on sticks. But we wouldn't eat too much, because we would save our appetites for Nathan's, the best hot dog, french fries, and corn-on-the-cob stand in the world. At Nathan's, the hot dogs were extra long and delicious, the french fries thick, tasty, and cut in a special wrinkled way that made them like no other french fries anywhere in the world.

Years later, as an adult, I came back to Coney Island. It seemed crowded, dirty, and noisy. I had no desire to go on those rides like the roller coaster that just make you dizzy and give you an upset stomach. The french fries at Nathan's seemed greasy. I had become a grown-up.

for Chapter 2   Mary Ellen Fischer

Mary Ellen Fischer was a special person to me when I was in the fourth grade. This may seem strange since I'm not sure I ever talked to her. What was special was that I was in love with her. I'm not sure what it was about her that made me fall in love. She was, I think, the prettiest girl in my class. She was rather quiet and shy, like me. Maybe it was that the biggest boy in the class, Marty Warner (who was also the best athlete), liked Mary Ellen. For whatever reason, I loved Mary Ellen. I used to daydream about taking her to parties (I didn't go on dates in the fourth grade, just to parties), about walking in the street near her house and just, by chance, meeting her and starting to talk to her. The song "On the Street Where You Live" would run through my mind. Of course, I never actually met Mary Ellen on the street, and I never did take her to parties, and she never did become my real girlfriend. That was fortunate. I wasn't ready for a real girlfriend in the fourth grade.

for Chapter 3   Learning to Drive

When I was sixteen years old, I got a learner's permit to learn how to drive a car. I got the permit just before my family was going to the country for our summer vacation, so I started practicing driving on country roads. It should have been easy, since there wasn't much traffic on those quiet little country roads. One thing that wasn't easy about it was that my father proved to be a very nervous teacher, having himself learned to drive at a rather late age, and being himself quite ill at ease behind the wheel. "Don't go so fast!" "You're over too much to the left!" "You're over too much to the right!" rang in my ear.

Despite this, I was finally ready to take my driving test. I started by forgetting to put on my directional signal when I pulled out from the curb, and then ignored a stop sign at the first intersection I came to. Some performance! Of course, I failed. I took a few driving classes after that and finally passed the test in New York City. I'll always remember my first summer of driving in New York—cabs honking their horns, cars speeding up behind me, no one very eager to let me pull onto a road or change lanes. After a while, though, I screwed up my courage, said to myself, "They're going to have to let me change lanes or hit me!" and started driving like a New Yorker.

for Chapter 4   Mr. Shaw—My English Teacher

I'll always remember Mr. Shaw, my best high-school English teacher. One of the greatest writers of all time is a Shaw—George Bernard Shaw. My high school teacher wasn't George Bernard Shaw, but he still seemed great to me, at least as great as George Bernard Shaw. It's hard to say exactly what was greatest about him. One thing was his love of words. He loved to talk himself, and appreciated it when students used words well. I remember him saying "Try to use words that produce an image, like 'copper pennies on a white marble table.'" Those copper pennies may not have been the greatest image in the world, but they have stayed in my mind to this day, and challenged me to do as well or better in my own use of words. And then he loved books. In his class, we didn't use a textbook—a heavy, ragged hard-covered thing with the names and marks of its previous victims scribbled on the inside. We used paperback books. I remember the excitement of seeing a carton of new, crisp, colorful paperbacks on Mr. Shaw's desk, and of feeling the fresh, portable prize in my hand. And they were good books, exciting stories, made more exciting by our lively class discussions and essays (students used to write in those days). Then there was that air of mystery about Mr. Shaw—it was said that he had been a college teacher, that he had lived abroad, that he had married an Oriental woman. And it was known that he had been seen, on numerous occasions, talking to quite a few of the lady teachers, who, it was assumed, doubtlessly found him irresistible, just as all the students did. Mr. Shaw, George Bernard Shaw could never compare with you!

for Chapter 5   School Has Not Been Useful to Me

When I look back on the years I spent in school, I don't remember feeling that I had a purpose for being there. I was there because I had to be there. My elementary school teachers seemed more like babysitters than teachers; in fact, I don't remember learning anything from them. I loved to read as a child and I believe I got some sort of education, more than anything else, from reading on my own. In junior high school and high school, my teachers at least seemed to know something about a particular subject, but it wasn't usually a subject that I cared to know about. I had no clear career goal and very few teachers communicated to me a good reason for learning what they were "teaching," other than "Learn it because I'm telling you to learn it!" or "Learn it or else you'll fail the test!" The few teachers that I liked, and that I learned from, were those rare individuals who seemed to have a real love for their subject, and who seemed to be excited about teaching it. I gradually began to lose my love of reading as my "education" progressed. Now, I have finished my "education," and I feel that my love of reading, and of learning, is gradually returning. I'm glad to see that the negative effect I experienced from being in school was only temporary.

for Chapter 6   Advantages of Being a Teacher

I come from a family of teachers. My father was a teacher, my sister is a teacher, and I am a teacher. What do we all find satisfying about this profession?

Well, for one thing, I consider myself not only a teacher, but also a learner. Being a teacher allows me, in fact forces me, to be a learner. I must find interesting articles or books for my students to read and write about. I must read and react to these books and articles myself in order to have something to share with my students. I must find ways of helping my students to understand their assignments. I must then try to understand and respond in a helpful way to my students' ideas.

A teacher's job is not, or does not need to be, routine. If you find yourself bored with doing the same thing over and over again, you have only yourself to blame. This is because a teacher has a great deal more independence and control over what he does than many other professionals do. In a sense, you are "king" in your classroom; only occasionally does a supervisor trespass into your territory and check on what you're doing. And again, you are almost forced to be creative, because if you deliver a boring, lifeless lesson, your students will let you know.

Teaching is also a "people job." It involves interacting with students and helping them to interact with each other. I suppose it doesn't have to be this way; a teacher can deliver a lecture and do nothing to find out whether anyone has understood what he said. But I question whether this is really teaching. A real teacher will make his ideas alive, and will awaken ideas in the minds of his students. In the process, he will benefit by getting to know his students as people—their past, their present, their ways of feeling and of thinking.

In sum, there is a great deal one can get out of being a teacher. I suppose not all teachers get all that they can out of their profession. Some may get very little. But for those who are suited by temperament to be teachers, it is a perfect job.

for Chapter 7   How Important Is Money?

No one would argue, I think, that money is unimportant. There are certain things that human beings need—food, shelter, perhaps medical care—and these things cost money. But if one has enough money to live on, to pay for the basic essentials of life, is it important to have a lot more money than that? Will your life improve in proportion to the amount of money that you have?

Well, there is no denying that money can buy a lot. Maybe you don't need much money to pay for simple shelter, but how about if you want a nice, big apartment in a nice neighborhood, or if you want to buy a house? The fact is that people do get on each other's nerves if they are crowded together in a small space, and that a married couple or members of a family are likely to get along better if they are not constantly tripping over each other and asking each other to not be so noisy—if each can find a little privacy from time to time. A big apartment or a house will allow them this privacy.

It's nice to get a little pleasure out of life, a little fun from time to time. Unfortunately, many of the fun things that you can do today cost money. New York City, for example, is one of the entertainment capitals of the world. On any night, outstanding performers appear in its clubs and on its concert stages. It is also a center of theater. Furthermore, you can dine on foods from every corner of the world in its countless restaurants. So how can it be that some people in New York don't have fun? Simple. They don't have the money to take advantage of all these attractions.

So, is money the road to happiness? Not really. Large numbers of people work every day, work overtime, work weekends, and make a lot of money. Are they happy? No. They're too busy working. Meanwhile, their personal lives, if they have any, fall apart; they have no time to form or to maintain friendships; they even lose the capacity to relax and enjoy themselves. Enjoying means taking things in, taking the time to see, to hear, to taste, to smell, to feel. Too many people do not take the time to do this. They say, "I'll do it when I have time" or "I'll do it when I have a vacation" (which rarely if ever comes) or "I'll do it when I make enough money to retire." Then they find that it is too late.

Surely everyone has thought at times, "If I only had a lot of money, I could be the happiest person in the world." It is important to remember, however, that money is only a means to an end, not the end itself.

for Chapter 8   Fighting Crime

Certainly one of the problems that anyone living in New York City has to be concerned about is crime. Every time you turn on the radio or look through the newspaper, you hear about muggings, murders, rapes, burglaries. It makes you feel like not turning on the radio. However, instead of trying to pretend that this problem doesn't exist, you're better off trying to do something about it.

Much can be done at the neighborhood level to control crime. On my block—in Park Slope, Brooklyn—we have an active block association that has had some success in fighting crime. One thing we have done is to get in touch with the local police precinct. Many people say of the police, "They're never there when you need them," and doubt whether policemen are very interested in fighting crime. I believe this isn't fair to the police. There are very few policemen in New York, and they can't show up everywhere at the same time. They have to work on a system of priorities, for example, going to the scene of a possible murder before going to a possible burglary. Members of my block association have gone to local police precinct meetings. The police have come to our block and given us suggestions about watching out for burglars and making the block safer. Since the police know us, they may tend to respond more quickly if we call them, and to believe that it is a real call for help rather than a false alarm.

Individual homeowners can do a lot by simply not making their houses easy to break into. Members of our block did an informal survey and found out that the majority of attempted break-ins were through the roof hatches on the flat roofs of our brownstone houses (where burglars can easily walk up and down, unseen by people in the streets). We walked up and down the roofs ourselves, and we informed people if they needed new, stronger roof hatches. In this area, as in medicine, "Prevention is the best cure."

Getting involved is better than hiding your head in the sand. When you come to think of it, there are a lot more law-abiding citizens than there are burglars. If the law-abiding citizens can only get together, the burglars don't stand a chance.

for Chapter 9   Comparing Menzel Bourguiba and New York City

After I finished college, I joined the U.S. Peace Corps, a volunteer organization aimed at aiding undeveloped countries, and went off to teach English in Tunisia, North Africa, for two years. I was assigned to a fairly small town in northern Tunisia called Menzel Bourguiba. Having grown up and lived most of my life in New York City, this was quite a change.

One great thing about Tunisia is that it is surrounded by the Mediterranean. I wasn't living far from the sea when I was there, and I spent a lot of time lying on the clean, white sand and lazily floating in the clear, warm, blue-green waters. My memories of going to the beach in New York were of dirty sand covered with paper cups, empty soda cans, broken bottles that would cut your feet if you didn't look out, blankets closely crowded together, beach umbrellas so thick you couldn't see the sky, radios blaring five different kinds of music all at the same time. At the Tunisian beaches, I was amazed at the comparative peace.

And the pace of life was so much slower and more pleasant in Tunisia. I used to sit in a cafe at the end of a day of teaching, and just stay there for hours and hours. Friends would come and go. We might decide to go eat in a restaurant, or to go to a movie, or just to sit there and chat. In New York, people don't usually do that. Everyone is always going somewhere, and is usually late. Why, if you tried walking slowly in the streets, you'd be run over by the mad hordes. Even if you find a cafe to sit in (there are a few in Greenwich Village and tucked away in other hard-to-find corners of the city), chances are that you will be looking at your watch and worrying about being late for a movie, or about being late for the babysitter. It seems that rush and worry are just in the air.

Living in Tunisia for a few years was a great experience for me. A friend of mine used to say, "You know, by living here for two years, I'll bet we are adding ten years to our lives." I don't know if that is true, but I do know that when I see New Yorkers madly running to get somewhere, or when I find myself doing this, I try to remind myself that life doesn't have to be like that.

for Chapter 10   Childlessness Is Not a Good Idea

In *Future Shock,* Alvin Toffler says "we may expect many among the people of the future to carry the streamlining process a step further by remaining childless." Because of this, Toffler points out, it will be more convenient for these couples to move around to different jobs in different locations. They will not be, as he puts it, "child-cluttered" families. But is convenience all that a couple should be aiming for? And are children mainly a "clutter" in our lives? If our society is in fact heading toward childlessness for the majority of married couples, perhaps we should pause to think about where we are going, and if we truly want to go there.

Having children is one of the great joys of life. Personally, before having children, I felt that I was beginning to get rather "middle-aged." I was busy working, making money, meeting my "responsibilities." When I had children, I began to see the world through their eyes. Everything was new, exciting, full of mystery and joy. The mystery of language began to unfold for them. They were always exploring, touching, trying to understand how things worked, asking questions. Nothing is boring to children. I found myself laughing more, seeing my children delighting in climbing a tree, jumping in the water, having their hair blow in the wind, catching, or even missing, a ball thrown to them. I rediscovered the delight of children's books in reading them to my own children, taking at least as much pleasure in them as my children did.

My wife and I also became friendly with other couples who had children. There is a tendency for people living in New York apartments to not talk to or get to know their neighbors. But children don't observe such barriers. Couples with children invited our children to their house and we invited their children to ours. We discussed how the children played together, what they were learning, how they liked school. We joined other parents in sitting around in playgrounds, going on family picnics, going to special children's plays or concerts. Raising children thus became a community effort, and we became a part of the community.

Having children has added a great deal to my life. Granted, it has not always been easy to work and to have children at the same time. Our society could do more to make this easier. But my life would surely be less happy if I had taken the "easy" route of not having children.

for Chapter 11 People Do Not Follow the Principles of Their Religion

The religions of the world have produced great books, with great lessons to teach. If we followed what is written in the books, the world would certainly be a better place. Unfortunately, most people, even so-called "religious" people, do not truly follow the paths of goodness and righteousness so beautifully described by their religion.

To many people in the United States, the house of worship (church, synagogue, etc.) is more a place to socialize than anything else. They come to see and to talk to their friends, to show off their fine clothes. They come because "people would talk" if they didn't come. They come to be entertained by the minister or rabbi, who tells interesting stories and reads beautiful words, or to hear the beautiful songs of the chorus. They come to eat, drink, and be merry. They do not come to learn how to live a better life.

Sometimes going to church can confirm one's feelings of pride. People are told of the great history of their group, of how their group suffered hardship in the past, but eventually prevailed over the enemy. They are congratulated on the good they have done and on the good their church has done. They contribute money to feed one hungry family in Africa or to pay for a scholarship so that one poor child can go to the country for a summer, and they feel reassured that they have done all that they should to make the world a better place.

But if one opens one's eyes, one sees poverty, crime, injustice throughout the world. If one looks inward, one may see selfishness, insensitivity, jealousy. If we saw these things more clearly, and understood their consequences, perhaps we could do more to eliminate them. But we do not ask our churches to open our eyes.

for Chapter 12   The Lives of Old People in the United States

In some countries, old people are revered, greatly respected, valued. This makes sense when you think about it. Having lived so many years, old people have accumulated a good bit of wisdom about life, not to mention a lot of good stories that they can share. Unfortunately, this is not the situation that exists in the United States.

Old people often don't have much of a life in the United States. This is particularly true in the cities. Many old people, not having much money, can't afford to live in big apartments or in good neighborhoods. So they stay locked up in small rooms, watching television, cleaning up, and thinking about the good old days. Their apartments are often located in neighborhoods where there is a lot of crime, so they are afraid to go out at night, nervous even about going out during the day, and, if they stay in, worried that a burglar may try to break into their apartment. Not much fun!

One of the pleasures of old age is spending time with grown-up sons and daughters, with grandsons and granddaughters. Yet the sons and daughters of old people in the United States are often not even living in the same city as their parents. They may only come to visit once or twice a year. Even if the sons and daughters are living in the same city, they are probably so busy that they don't have time to visit or to call very often.

Some old people in the United States have moved to special "retirement communities." In these communities, they spend time socializing, playing games, going to classes, relaxing. There is no problem about finding people to talk to or to do things with because everyone has a lot of free time and is open to forming friendships or to getting involved in new activities. The old people maintain contact with their sons and daughters, but they do not depend on their sons and daughters for company. This life style seems to work pretty well for those old people who can afford it (life in these communities isn't cheap).

In sum, the United States doesn't offer much of a life to its "senior citizens." Despite this, at least some of the elderly have managed to make a good life for themselves.

for Chapter 13   What I Want to Accomplish in Life

I just had my thirty-sixth birthday. When I was in my twenties, I thought people were getting old, or at least middle-aged, when they were in their thirties. Fortunately, now that I am in my thirties, this seems quite young to me; now I would say that you don't start getting old till you're in your forties. But whether I am in fact getting old or not doesn't bother me very much. I think this is because I am happy with the way my life is going and I feel that I am achieving the goals that are important to me.

One of my goals is to build a good family life—a good relationship with my wife and my children. My wife and I have worked together to raise kids, fix up a house, develop a social life, develop careers. It hasn't been easy but I feel that we're doing well. We share the work, enjoy the kids, and still enjoy spending time with each other. I feel more fortunate than many men in that I have been able to spend a lot of time with my two daughters. We have shared a lot of good times, have gotten used to being together, and have really gotten to like each other quite a bit over the years. I consider them to be two good friends.

It's important to have meaningful work. I feel fortunate that I have found a job which is so well suited to my temperament as teaching. I get great pleasure from seeing my students learn. I enjoy helping them to appreciate the mysteries and beauties of language. I grow as a person by relating to my students and helping them to relate to each other. A classroom can be a place, I feel, where growth, for both teacher and student, can go on forever. I hope to make my classroom such a place.

You might be tempted to hide away from the world these days, especially when you hear about all the crimes reported on the radio. College professors, in fact, are known for hiding away in their "ivory towers," formulating theories that may have little to do with the real world. This is not the way that I want to live and it is not the way that I am living. I am involved with my neighbors, with my block association, with my children's schools, with community groups. I try to be aware of the world outside and I hope in the future to become more involved, to find ways that I can help to make this a better world.

I don't know if I will be able to look back on my life at the end and to feel satisfied with it, to feel that it was good. Right now though, it seems likely to me that I will.

RHETORICAL CHECKLIST

1. Is there an interesting *introduction,* with introductory comments and with a *thesis* (see page 54)? See the suggestions for writing different types of introductions on page 96.

2. Are there separate *middle paragraphs,* each with a main idea and *examples, explanation, details* (not just generalities)?

3. Is there an interesting *conclusion,* with the *thesis repeated* (not using the same words as in the introduction) and with concluding comments? See the suggestions for writing different types of conclusions on page 98.

GRAMMATICAL CHECKLIST

correction symbols*

art.	article (*a/an, the*)
comb.	combine two sentences (using coordination, subordination, a sentence connector, or an adjective clause)
compar.	comparative form
conn.	connecting word needed
dic.	idiomatic diction error (wrong word or expression)

---

*These are suggested symbols. Your teacher's symbols may not be the same.

frag.	fragment (not a complete sentence)
n.pl.	plural noun needed
n.sg.	singular noun needed
poss.	possessive form
prep.	preposition
pron.	pronoun error
punc.	punctuation
run-on	run-on sentence (should be two sentences)
sp.	spelling
s.s.	sentence structure (wrong word order, word omitted, sentence not correctly connected)
sup.	superlative form
S-V agr.	subject-verb agreement
t.	wrong verb tense used
v. form	wrong verb form (present participle, past participle, infinitive, gerund)
v.pl.	plural verb needed (error in S-V agreement)
v.sg.	singular verb needed (error in S-V agreement)
w. form	wrong word form
ℒ	omit this
‖ struct.	parallel structure needed
∧	something is missing

COPYRIGHTS AND ACKNOWLEDGMENTS

For permission to use the excerpts reprinted in this book, the author is grateful to the following publishers and copyright holders:

THE DIAL PRESS   From "Choosing A Dream: Italians in Hell's Kitchen" by Mario Puzo and "Time and Tide" by John A. Williams from *The Immigrant Experience: The Anguish of Becoming American* edited by Thomas Wheeler. Copyright © 1971 by The Dial Press. Permission granted by The Dial Press.

FOREIGN POLICY ASSOCIATION   From "Teaching about Spaceship Earth" by Donald Morris, a chapter in *International Education for Spaceship Earth,* #4 of the New Dimensions series. Copyright 1970 by the Foreign Policy Association.

HARPER & ROW, PUBLISHERS, INC.   For "Brotherly Love" (pp. 47–48) from *The Art of Loving* by Erich Fromm. Volume Nine of the World Perspective series edited by Ruth Nanda Anshen. Copyright © 1956 by Erich Fromm. For the specified excerpt from "Education" from *One Man's Meat* by E. B. White. Copyright 1939 by E. B. White. All reprinted by permission of Harper & Row, Publishers, Inc.

HOUGHTON MIFFLIN COMPANY   For Carl R. Rogers: *On Becoming a Person,* p. 281. Copyright © 1961 Houghton Mifflin Company. Used by permission.

ELISABETH KÜBLER-ROSS, M.D.   From "Facing Up to Death" by Elisabeth Kübler-Ross from *Today's Education,* January 1972. Reprinted by permission.

HAROLD MATSON COMPANY, INC.   From "Dirt, Grime, and Cruel Crowding" by Eric Sevareid, from the Philadelphia *Evening Bulletin,* July 8, 1962. Copyright © 1962 by Eric Sevareid. Used by permission.

WILLIAM MORROW & COMPANY, INC.   From pp. 42–44 "The way in which . . . children's early adulthood." and from pp. 45–46 "My paternal grandmother . . . voice that it was necessary." in *Blackberry Winter: My Earlier Years* by Margaret Mead. Copyright © 1972 by Margaret Mead. By permission of William Morrow & Company.

MS. FOUNDATION FOR EDUCATION & COMMUNICATION, INC.   From "Measuring Masculinity by the Size of a Paycheck" by Robert E. Gould from *Ms.,* July 1973. Copyright Ms. Foundation for Education & Communication, Inc., 1973. Reprinted with permission.

RANDOM HOUSE, INC.   Specified excerpt from pp. 17–19 from *Growing Up Absurd* by Paul Goodman. Copyright © 1960 by Paul Goodman. Specified excerpt from pp. 241–243 from *Future Shock* by Alvin Toffler. Copyright © 1970 by Alvin Toffler. Both reprinted by permission of Random House, Inc.

PICTURE CREDITS

p. 2, © George W. Gardner;   p. 12, Library of Congress, reprinted from *Blackberry Winter* by permission of M. C. Bateson;   p. 22, © Jeff Albertson/Stock, Boston;   p. 32, © Paul Conklin;   p. 42, © Robert Kingman/Photo Researchers, Inc.;   p. 52, © Mark Antman/The Image Works;   p. 62, © Rick Smolan/Stock, Boston;   p. 72, © Michael D. Sullivan;   p. 80, © George W. Gardner;   p. 90, © Peter Southwick/Stock, Boston;   p. 100, © Michael D. Sullivan;   p. 110, © Robert V. Eckert, Jr./EKM-Nepenthe;   p. 120, Library of Congress, reprinted from *Blackberry Winter* by permission of M. C. Bateson.

INDEX OF RHETORICAL AND GRAMMATICAL TOPICS

A

A/an, 57–58
Adjective clauses, 25
Adjectives,
   comparative forms of, 85–86
   descriptive, 4
   superlative forms of, 85–86
Adverbs, comparative forms of, 85
Appositives, 27
Argumentative
   essay, 53–54, 61, 63–64
   paragraph, 49
Articles,
   (a/an) indefinite, 57
   (the) definite, 58

C

Classification essay, 91–92, 111–112
Clauses, restrictive and nonrestrictive, 26
Cohesion (see Connecting expressions)
Comparing with adjectives and adverbs,
   85–86

Comparison/contrast essay, 81–82, 88
Conclusion essay, 56, 98
Conditional sentences, 104–105
Connecting expressions:
   addition, 16
   comparison, 17
   contrast, 17
   emphasis, 17
   explanation, 17
   illustration, 17
   order, 17
   result, 17
   time, 17
Coordination, sentence, 15–16

D

Definite article, 58–59
Definition essay, 102
Descriptive
   essay, 121
   passages, 3–4, 10, 13–14, 73–74
   words, 4, 14, 35, 123
Direct speech and reported speech,
   86–87

E

Essays,
 classification of, 91–92, 111–112
 conclusions of, 96–98
 formal, 53–54
 introductions of, 96–98
 parts of, 54–56

F

Formal essay, 53–54
Fragments, 6

G

Gerunds, 115
 conventional uses of, 115–116
Grammatical checklist, 138–139

I

Infinitives, 115
 conventional uses of, 115–116
Introductions, essay, 54

M

Middle paragraphs, essay, 54
Modal verbs, 94–95
Model passages or essays, 131–138

N

Narrative passage or paragraph, 23, 28,
 121
Noun phrases, 116–117

O

Omitting the connecting word, 27
Opinion and support
 essays or passages, 53, 63
 paragraph, 43, 49
Other perfect tenses, 48

P

Parallel structure, 124–125
Passive verb forms, 76
Past perfect tense (*see* Other perfect
 tenses)
Present perfect tense, 47
Present perfect continuous tense (*see*
 Other perfect tenses)
Problem solution essay, 78
Pronoun
 agreement, 38–39
 reference, 39–40
Punctuation, 8–9

Q

Questions used in essays, 97
Quotes used in essays, 98

R

Reported speech, direct speech and, 86
Restrictive and nonrestrictive clauses, 27
Rhetorical
 checklist, 138
 devices, 4, 14, 24, 34–35, 44, 56,
  64–65, 74, 83, 93, 103, 113, 123
Run-on sentences, 7

S

Sample writing passages, 131–138
Sentence
 connectors (*see* Connecting
  expressions)
 coordination, 15–16
 fragments, 6
 variety, 68
Sentences,
 combining, 15
 complete, 5
 run-on, 7
Subject-verb agreement, 36–38
 special rules, 37–38
Subordination:
 comparison, 18

condition, 19
contrast, 19
manner, 19
place, 18
purpose, 18
reason, 18
result, 19
time, 18
Superlative, 85

T

Tenses, 45
Thesis sentence, 54
Topic sentence, 34, 54
Transition (*see* Connecting expressions)

V

Verb tenses, 45–46, 47, 48
Verbs,
    and agreement with
    subject, 36 – 38
    passive forms of, 76
Verbals:
    gerunds, 115
    infinitives, 115

W

Word forms, 66
Wordiness, 125–126

A 3
B 4
C 5
D 6
E 7
F 8
G 9
H 0
I 1
J 2